A Bit About
Britain's History
From a long time ago until quite recently

Mike Biles

Copyright © 2019 M W G Biles
All rights reserved.
ISBN: 978-1-0887-2528-3

To Carole – it wouldn't have happened without you.

CONTENTS

	Author's Note	vii
	Britain	viii
1	ANCIENT BRITAIN	1
	Prehistory	1
	Roman Britain	5
2	EARLY MEDIEVAL BRITAIN	10
	Dark Age Britain	10
	Christianity and the age of saints	15
	Newsflash! Vikings murder defenceless monks	20
	Why London is the capital of Britain	25
	How the Normans shaped world history	29
3	LATER MEDIEVAL BRITAIN	34
	Brits invent parliamentary democracy	34
	How Scotland was born	38
	Whatever happened to Wales?	43
	Why France isn't part of Britain	45
	When death walked the land	51
	A violent royal soap opera	54
4	THE TUDORS	60
	The victor of Bosworth	60
	Losing our religion	63
	Dawn of Empire	69
5	THE STUARTS	75
	The Stuarts and the Republic	75
	Restoration and Glorious Revolution	83
	When Britain got a German king	89
6	GEORGIAN (or HANOVERIAN) BRITAIN	92
	The last battle	92
	British expansion	100
	Why they don't play cricket (much) in the USA	105
	Britain's industrial revolution	110
	"The greatest happiness of the greatest number"	117
	Revolting Britain	120
	How Britain got the vote	124

7	VICTORIAN BRITAIN	127
	Wasn't the Victorian era great?	127
	Poor Britain	133
	The Empire on which the sun never set	136
8	EDWARDIAN BRITAIN	140
	Fog in Channel – Europe cut off	140
	How did the First World War happen?	145
9	MODERN BRITAIN	156
	Britain & the First World War	156
	The legacy of 1914-18	161
	What happened in the 1920s & 1930s?	166
	Could Britain have avoided war in 1939?	170
	Britain and the Second World War	173
	Britain after 1945	182
	TIMELINES	189
	I - Prehistoric Timeline	190
	II - Roman Timeline	192
	III - Early Medieval Timeline	195
	IV – Later Medieval Timeline	201
	V – Tudor Timeline	208
	VI – Stuart Timeline	215
	VII – Georgian, or Hanoverian, Timeline	222
	VIII – Victorian Timeline	231
	IX – Edwardian Timeline	240
	X – Modern Timeline 1914-1945	244
	XI – Modern Timeline – 1945 - 2000	252
	Note on sources and further reading	265
	About the author	266

AUTHOR'S NOTE

The past is us. It was also so totally different from anything you have experienced.

A Bit About Britain's History began as a series of online articles, because I needed historical background for the A Bit About Britain website. This features heritage and other attractions and the history puts places, people and things in context. Gradually, you start seeing how everything joins up. Then I realised there may be a gap for a little book that told Britain's amazing story in a light way, without appearing to be a heavy academic tome at one extreme, or a comic romp at the other; something that covers the basic hows and whys, that can be read relatively easily from start to finish, or dipped into - maybe even used for reference.

So this book pulls the web content into a single volume and is organised chronologically into nine periods of British history, with articles about selected key events or themes along the way. At the end are timelines for each period, which provide useful reference but also make fascinating reading in their own right. A Bit About Britain's History provides an understanding of how Britain evolved, a picture of the long meandering path that stretches behind us. It really is quite a tale, from man's first footsteps across a land that is now under the sea, to the digital age. If the book inspires a love of history, or a desire to delve into more detailed works written by much more serious professional historians, then I'll be a happy bunny.

You have to be highly selective when compiling a book like this: what to include; what to leave out? Of course, the interpretation and emphasis of history can be a matter of opinion; and this is mine – as is the responsibility for any errors, factual or otherwise. Enjoy!

BRITAIN

Britain is an island in the North Atlantic, off the coast of western Europe. It is the largest of a group of about 6,000 islands, the British Isles. The island of Britain contains the nations of England, Wales, and Scotland. The three nations together form a political entity, Great Britain, which also includes several islands belonging to those nations. 'Great Britain' is commonly abbreviated to simply 'Britain', but both terms are used in a geographical as well as a political sense.

The nations of Great Britain are part of a sovereign state which includes Northern Ireland. This is the United Kingdom, or 'UK' - full name 'the United Kingdom of Great Britain and Northern Ireland'.

The inhabitants of Britain and the United Kingdom are generally referred to as 'British', or specifically from their country of origin – English, Scottish, Welsh or Northern Irish.

A Bit About Britain's History

1 ANCIENT BRITAIN

Prehistory

From nothing to the Roman occupation

Once upon a very long time ago, but not necessarily at the same time, Britain was inhabited by extremely large lizards, woolly rhinos, mammoths, sabre-toothed tigers, giant cattle called aurochs, enormous bears, deer with antlers as long as a person – indeed, all manner of wild animals not often spotted on your local High Street. Our distant ancestors would not have been familiar with dinosaurs, which died out around 65 million years ago; but they would have known those other vanished creatures – perhaps, with the assistance of a changing climate, helping to drive some to extinction. Though 'A Bit About Britain's History' concentrates on the relatively recent events that took place over the last couple of millennia, of course the wider human story begins much, much earlier than that.

It is reckoned that the first primitive primates evolved about 55 million years ago, the first true hunter-gatherer, *Homo Erectus*, walked the earth about 1-2 million years ago (give or take) and the direct ancestor of modern man, *Homo Sapiens*, made an appearance a mere 195,000 years or so before you arrived. The first evidence of a humanoid presence in Britain itself goes back about 700-800,000 years, to primitive hunter-gatherers who left their tools, and their footprints, in the tidal muds at Happisburgh, Norfolk. These were the earliest northern Europeans identified so far. They were not humans as we know them, however; they weren't even like politicians. The oldest human remains found in Britain to date are those of so-called Boxgrove Man; parts of a fossilised tibia and a couple of teeth uncovered at a site in West Sussex have been dated at about half a million years old and belong to an extinct species, Heidelberg Man (*Homo heidelbergensis*). The partial skull of Swanscombe Man (or, probably, Swanscombe Woman), discovered up the road in Kent is slightly younger – perhaps 350,000 BC.

Modern Homo Sapiens arrived in Britain much more recently, about 25,000 years back, though climatic changes probably meant that occupation did not become permanent until perhaps 12-10,000 BC. The last ice age, around 10,000 years ago, covered Britain in ice down to a little south of the English Midlands. At that time Britain was not an island, but physically joined to continental Europe across what is now the North Sea. This drowned land, known as 'Doggerland', is believed to have been fertile and possibly relatively well-populated. It gradually gave way to the rising sea as the ice melted around 8,000 years ago (6,000 BC), and the land adjusted through a process of isostatic rebounding as the weight of the ice was removed, leaving the last land bridge somewhere in the region of East Anglia and Kent; eventually, that too was inundated. It is doubtful whether the significance of the event was widely recognised at the time – possibly the original hard Brexit. Experts tell us that the highest part of Doggerland, Dogger Bank, remained as an island until c5,000 BC, when it was finally overwhelmed by an enormous tsunami created by a volcanic eruption off the coast of Norway.

The Neolithic Period (the new, or later, Stone Age) in Britain, from around 4,500 BC, saw permanent settlements, farming and the use of stone tools. Long barrows – burial chambers – were built from around 3,700 BC and are among the oldest surviving structures in the country. They seem to have been communal graves. From about 3,300 BC, our ancestors built stone circles and 'henges' (usually an earthwork with a ditch). There are at least 1,000 stone circles in Britain, along with a plethora of other stone monuments, including single megaliths, aligned stones and avenues.

The Bronze Age in Britain seems to have been introduced by the so-called 'Beaker People', migrants characterised by their bell-shaped pottery who arrived sometime around 2,000 BC and who buried their dead in individual round barrows. Hill forts were also built in the Bronze Age - the remains of more than 2,000 of them punctuate Britain's landscape today. The first hill fort was built about 3,500 years ago (1500 BC), though most date from the Iron Age (about 750 BC). Broadly speaking, development spread into Britain from continental Europe and was therefore generally slower in the north of the island, further from these influences. We know that there was regular contact with mainland Europe, and the discovery of intricately fashioned gold torcs (decorative neck rings) in a field in Staffordshire in 2016 suggests sophisticated trade or social exchange. The torcs have been dated to perhaps 400 BC and are thought to have originated from what is now France or Germany. The largest collection of Iron Age gold, silver and bronze artefacts found in Europe to date has been uncovered over a 60 year period at Snettisham, Norfolk. Dating from c70 BC, the Snettisham Treasure includes beautiful, complete, items of jewellery as well as fragments, coins and ingots.

By the later part of the Iron Age, just prior to the Roman conquest (43 AD), the predominant culture in the British Isles was Celtic, apart from a significant portion of Scotland, which was occupied by the Picts - who may, or may not, have been ethnically Celtic. The Celts migrated to these islands over a long period of time, probably from central Europe, and are still here in places; the Picts aren't. We know very little of the Picts – the name comes from the Latin meaning 'painted people' – and they disappear from our story, along with their language and culture, after being absorbed by the Scots in the 9th century AD. In any event, immediately before the Roman invasion, the people of

Britain were probably tribal, but highly organised. They lived in farmsteads or villages, perhaps surrounded by a fence or wall. We don't know what they called themselves. The only written references to them comes from the Roman writers, Ptolemy and Tacitus, and it is through them that we hear of tribes such as the *Durotriges* in modern Dorset/Wiltshire, the *Atrebates* in parts of Sussex, Hampshire and Berkshire, the *Iceni* in Norfolk and Suffolk, the *Brigantes* in Yorkshire, Durham and Lancashire, the *Votadini* in south east Scotland, the *Caledones* in the Highlands - and the Picts in the north east.

For thousands of years before the written word, generations of people lived their lives in Britain; they were born, had their childhood, grew to adulthood, worked, died and made their mark on the landscape. We may know little of their hopes and dreams – but they must have had them. They cleared vast tracts of forest and left behind hundreds of memorials to their endeavours - stone circles, burial chambers, hill forts, ancient settlements and trackways, giant figures carved into hillsides and strange standing stones. The purpose of many of these structures is unknown – but much debated. Their memory is also preserved in Britain's museums, which contain thousands of artefacts, ranging from primitive stone and bone tools, to exquisite and stylish Celtic jewellery.

Roman Britain

Apart from sanitation, medicine, education, wine, law, public order, irrigation, roads, a fresh water system, public health...

What did the Romans ever do for Britain? The answer to a similar question posed in the 1979 film 'Monty Python's Life of Brian' on the face of it seems to be, "rather a lot". Yet it is sometimes hard to believe that Britain was once part of the Roman world. The Romans conquered all of what is now England (the extent of Roman rule in Cornwall is disputed) and Wales (sort of), but never conquered Ireland or Scotland - though their armies did penetrate as far north as Aberdeenshire. Back then, '*Britannia*' was the northernmost province of an enormous empire that extended across most of central and southern Europe to North Africa, the Middle East and modern day Iran.

Do not think of the Roman Empire as a kind of early Italian superstate; for one thing, Italy as a unified nation state did not exist until 1870. Rome was a truly international civilisation encircling the Mediterranean, which the Romans called *Mare Nostrum* – our sea. The city of Rome, from which the Empire had grown, was its hub – though ultimately an eastern capital was established too, in the Greek town of Byzantium, later renamed Constantinople – modern Istanbul. Rome was also the soul of the Empire and had an almost mystical meaning to many of its citizens. Overall, the Roman Empire was a huge economic trading zone and way of life that embraced people if they wanted to play by its rules, irrespective of racial origins. It was undeniably hierarchical, and cruel. Perhaps 25%, maybe 30%, of its population were slaves, captured in war, bred in captivity, bought and sold; numbers varied according to time and place. But people could – and did – rise and fall through Rome's ranks and, sometimes, slaves were freed.

The Romans were in Britain for a long time - the best part of 400 years – equivalent to the period from the Stuart kings of England to the present day. By the time Roman rule petered out in the early 5th century, Britain south of Hadrian's Wall was a highly organised society used to Roman ways and laws. Though predominantly agrarian, it had a strong urban base, home to perhaps 10% of the population. Towns were centres of trade, politics, religion and administration and many modern British towns are built on Roman foundations. They often, but not always, have 'chester' in their names – like Manchester, Winchester, Colchester, Bath and Chester - from the Latin *castra* meaning a camp or fortified place. While most native Brits continued to live on the land, as they always had, the Romans introduced the people of Britain to brick and stone buildings, public baths, shops and theatres. The wealthy had country villas, or even palaces, with under floor heating, mosaics in the floor and glass in the windows. Of course, most of the hard work was done by the ubiquitous slaves, many of whom lived squalid, miserable lives.

Although the ancient Romans knew about the island of Britain before it became part of their Empire, and the tribes of Britain traded with mainland Europe, many Romans believed that the land was beyond the limits of the known world. The first direct Roman contact with Britain is thought to have been when Julius Caesar attacked in 55 BC. This was probably a punitive expedition against tribes who had been aiding his enemies across the Channel in Gaul (modern France and Belgium). On that occasion, he probably did not progress far beyond the boundaries of the modern county of Kent, but Caesar returned the following year with a fleet of 800 ships carrying thousands of troops. This time, he headed for the territory of the *Catuvellauni* north of the Thames, beat them and exacted a tribute. The Romans then left Britain alone for a hundred years, until 43 AD when the Emperor Claudius dispatched the General

Aulus Plautius with around 40,000 troops to conquer Britain properly. The Romans set about their task with typically ruthless efficiency, dispatching armies north toward the Humber, north-west to the Trent and west through south-east and south-west England. Despite fierce resistance, within about 5 years the Romans had established themselves in southern and central England.

Probably the most famous resistance came from Boudicca (also known as Boudica or Boadicea), Queen of the Iceni, in around 60 or 61 AD. Brutal treatment by the Romans, including the rape of Boudicca's daughters, resulted in a furious uprising. The hated Roman colony at Colchester was burnt to the ground, its inhabitants massacred. London came next, followed by St Albans. By this time, London was already a city of perhaps 10,000 citizens; the evidence of its destruction by Boudicca's army is revealed whenever archaeologists uncover a red and black layer of burnt material in the City. The Roman Governor, Suetonius Paulinus, gathered his forces and, at an unknown site somewhere in the English Midlands, the fate of Britain was decided. Though outnumbered by the Iceni and their allies, Roman discipline and weaponry prevailed and Britain continued as a province of the Empire. Boudicca committed suicide. The Romans also seem to have exterminated the Druids – the high priests of the Celts – most notably by destroying what was possibly a sacred centre on the island of Anglesey. By 80 AD, most of modern England and Wales had been pacified and the then Roman Governor, Agricola, decided to crush the wild tribes in what is now Scotland. He got as far as somewhere near Inverurie, fighting a pitched, victorious, battle against the Caledonians in c84 AD at a place history knows only as *Mons Graupius*.

Despite the briefly used Antonine Wall near the Clyde, traces of which remain, the border between Roman Britain and the restless tribes in the north was finally settled at

Hadrian's Wall, stretching more than 70 miles between the Solway Firth on the Irish Sea to the River Tyne near the North Sea, with forts every 5 miles and watch-towers in between. The Emperor Hadrian ordered the building of the Wall in 120 AD and it was finished by about 128. Outbreaks of violence were relatively frequent on both sides of the Wall. The northern British experience of Rome was generally more military in nature than in the south.

From sometime in the 3rd century, the frontiers of Rome came under increasing threat from the tribes beyond its borders. Britain itself was raided by Germanic Saxons and Franks and a series of defensive forts was built along the coast from Norfolk to Hampshire, known as the Saxon Shore. However, in 367 AD, simultaneous attacks – whether by chance or deliberate organisation is not known – took place: Scots and *Attacotti* (an elusive group of uncertain origin) swept east across the Irish Sea, Picts fell upon the Wall from the north and Saxons attacked the shore defences from the east. Deserters and escaped slaves joined in the anarchy, which lasted about a year until order was restored by the last of three generals, Theodosius, appointed by Rome to save the province.

Rural villas were particularly vulnerable to attack and there is grim evidence of this. There is further evidence that villas were gradually abandoned for safer life in towns. However, though Roman life went on, Roman rule in Britain was nearing its end. The Germanic tribes of Europe were on the move, themselves threatened by a violent Asiatic people, the Huns, who had appeared from the east. Early in the 5th century, Rome itself came under threat and troops were needed to preserve it; the Roman garrison in Britain departed. A last-ditch plea to the Emperor Honorius in 410 AD resulted in Britain being told to look to its own defence. Rome had its own problems; far away that same year, 410 AD, the imperial city itself fell to Alaric's Goths. To some, it must have seemed like the end of the world.

Alas, the successors to the Romans in Britain lacked the skills, or motivation, to maintain the civilisation they inherited. Moreover, they virtually eradicated the Romano-British way of life such that the extent of the Roman legacy in these islands (apart from rabbits) is debateable. Yet Roman towns lie beneath many modern British urban areas and their remains offer a tantalising glimpse of what must have been. Motorists and hikers may find themselves travelling on the same path that legionaries tramped along; indeed, stretches of modern roads follow routes mapped out by Roman engineers to facilitate military traffic, trade and communications almost two thousand years ago. Exotic mosaics lie on the floors of excavated villas, mainly in the south and west of England. In the city of Bath, which the Romans called *Aquae Sulis*, are the spectacular remains of the elegant Roman bath complex. The north and coastal areas of Britain offer the remains of forts, some of them very remote, like the one at Hardknott Pass in Cumbria; and the ruins of Hadrian's Wall provide spectacular scenery and walking as well as a dip into ancient heritage and fascinating glimpses into the lives of the people that once lived and worked there. Roman artefacts, from treasure to everyday objects, can be found in museums the length of the land, from the British Museum in London to more humble collections in provincial towns.

2 EARLY MEDIEVAL BRITAIN

Dark Age Britain

Romano-British culture is swept aside by foreign invaders

Some history books suggest that the Romans left Britain in 410 AD; full stop. This somehow conjures up a ludicrous vision of the Romans, suitcases packed, hopping on the first convenient galley from Dover to Calais - and that was it, everything fell apart and the next bunch of invaders, the Saxons, moved in. Though there must have been a finite moment when the last appointed official, or troop of soldiers, left – probably sometime in the early 5th century – Roman civilisation and influence in Britain declined gradually. Moreover, what remained was hardly a cultural backwater. In the space of almost four centuries, Roman society and organisation had become the way of life for most of mainland Britain south of Hadrian's Wall, and many of those who made it work would have been Romano-British who weren't planning on moving overseas anytime soon. It makes sense that the social order continued, at least for a while; and we know that it did, in places. However, there is also evidence of stone buildings falling into disrepair and only basic wood and thatch structures being built in their place.

Actually, though it didn't occur overnight, what happened to Britain next could be described as the most cataclysmic period in the island's history. It was so cataclysmic that we don't know terribly much about it – there are limited sources, and no contemporary ones. The events of the 5th and 6th centuries in Britain had a profound effect. Imagine this organised society, with towns, a judicial system, people happily taking stuff to market, meeting in the public baths for a gossip, craftsmen making mosaic floors, masons dressing stone for buildings and so on. Well, it completely disappeared; and what emerged was a rather different place where urban life became very basic and even a different language was spoken. The people that brought this about were the ancestors of the modern English.

Germanic pirates – Saxons, Angles, Jutes and Frisians (all often generally referred to as Saxons or 'Anglo-Saxons') – had been raiding Britain for years. The Roman Army had long used auxiliary troops from all parts of the Empire and, like all good imperialists, were adept at using mercenaries – some of which were probably Germanic tribesmen of one sort or another – to fight their battles. No doubt some of these mercenaries had settled, particularly in the south east, with their families. We do not know exactly what, or for how long, Roman-style governance lasted into the 5th century, but whatever rule of law remained had the task of dealing with the ongoing problem of land-hungry pirates. Some of these were almost certainly quick to exploit the opportunity that a perception of diminishing order presented. At the same time, there is the suggestion of pestilence and famine. The Benedictine monk, the Venerable Bede, albeit writing in the 8th century, says that the plague "destroyed so large a number that the living could not bury the dead."

It appears that local rulers tried to buy the raiders off – which seems about as sensible as offering a bribe to the local mafia. Conventional legend has it that a Romano-British chieftain, or king (we don't know which, but he is referred to as a *superbus tyrannus* by the 6th century monk, St Gildas), who was possibly called Vortigern, invited two Saxons blessed with the names Hengest and Horsa (stallion and horse) to serve as mercenaries to fight off assorted Picts, Scots (Irish) and other Saxons. Allegedly, this all went pear-shaped when they fell out over payment. So the mercenaries turned on their former employers, more joined in and, eventually, what had started as pirate raids ended up as permanent settlement.

The traditional view is that the Anglo-Saxon take-over ('invasion' somehow suggests coordinated action, which is doubtful, initially) was extremely violent, driving the surviving Romano-British westward into what is now Wales, Devon, Cornwall and Strathclyde – or out of these islands totally to Brittany ('Little', or 'Lesser', Britain). As more and more Saxons arrived, resistance stiffened. It is likely that this resistance was led by local warlords, who had filled the power vacuum left by the Romans, in the same way as happens in modern times when a strong centralised power is removed. We know that some Iron Age hilltop forts were re-occupied at this time. One of the leaders of this resistance is a shadowy figure called Ambrosius Aurelianus who, if he existed, may have had Roman ancestry. Legend has it that there was a series of 12 battles, culminating in the mysterious and illusive Battle of Badon around 500 AD, which resulted in a period of peace for 40 years or so. This is the period associated with the mythical figures of Uthur Pendragon, Merlin – and, of course, the legendary King Arthur with his probably non-existent knights of the round table.

What we do know is that within a hundred or so years of the Romans leaving, Anglo-Saxon kingdoms had been established, and these people came to dominate all of what is now modern England – though Devon and Cornwall (known as West Wales or *Dumnonia*) were not conquered until much later. In the north west of modern England, in and around modern Cumbria, was the territory of *Rheged*; beyond that, in what is now south west Scotland, lay the kingdom of the Strathclyde Welsh. What we know as modern Wales was also Celtic-British territory – the name Wales comes from the Anglo-Saxon *Wealas* (or variations of it), meaning 'strangers', or 'foreigners'. It was a term the Anglo-Saxons applied to people other than themselves. Today, the Welsh call themselves *Cymry*, and their country

Cymru; both words come from old Celtic, meaning something like 'fellow-countrymen'. But in the sub-Roman period, their country did not exist and consisted of a number of separate kingdoms such as Dyfed, Powys, Gwynedd and Gwent. The Saxons never conquered Wales or Scotland, though the much later Anglian Kingdom of Northumbria did include what is now south-east Scotland as far as the Firth of Forth.

So, apart from it being very inconvenient if you lived here, why was all of this so cataclysmic? The answer is that though Britons survived in Saxon territory, particularly in more remote areas, Germanic culture totally replaced the more technologically advanced Romano-British one. Notwithstanding the evident beauty of Saxon art and craftsmanship, civilisation essentially took a step backward. Celtic ceased to be the main spoken language of the people and very few Celtic, or 'British', place names have survived in England. One example is the hill Pen-y-Ghent in Yorkshire; another is the river Avon - but this is tautology; '*avon*' is Celtic for 'river'. Many Romano-British people were Christian: the Anglo-Saxons were not. As far as we know, Christianity died out in England, though it continued in parts of western Britain, until being more widely reintroduced from the late 6th century by St Columba from the north and St Augustine from the south. Even the Normans in 1066 didn't achieve the wholesale replacement of language and culture, though their impact on Britain was just as profound.

The Celtic Brits and the Anglo-Saxons continued to fight each other, and themselves, with the latter evolving kingdoms and administrative units that are still a part of the English landscape and local government today. Some names, however, such as *Deiria* and *Bernicia* (roughly equivalent to modern North Yorkshire and Northumberland), *Lyndsey* (Lincolnshire) and *Rheged* (Cumbria), have long disappeared from daily use. The

A Bit About Britain's History

Anglo-Saxon kingdoms morphed into seven main ones - Northumbria, Mercia, Kent, East Anglia, Essex, Sussex and Wessex (east, south and west Saxons respectively) – which vied with one another to be the most powerful in the land, their leaders aspiring to be *bretwalda* – chief ruler in Britain.

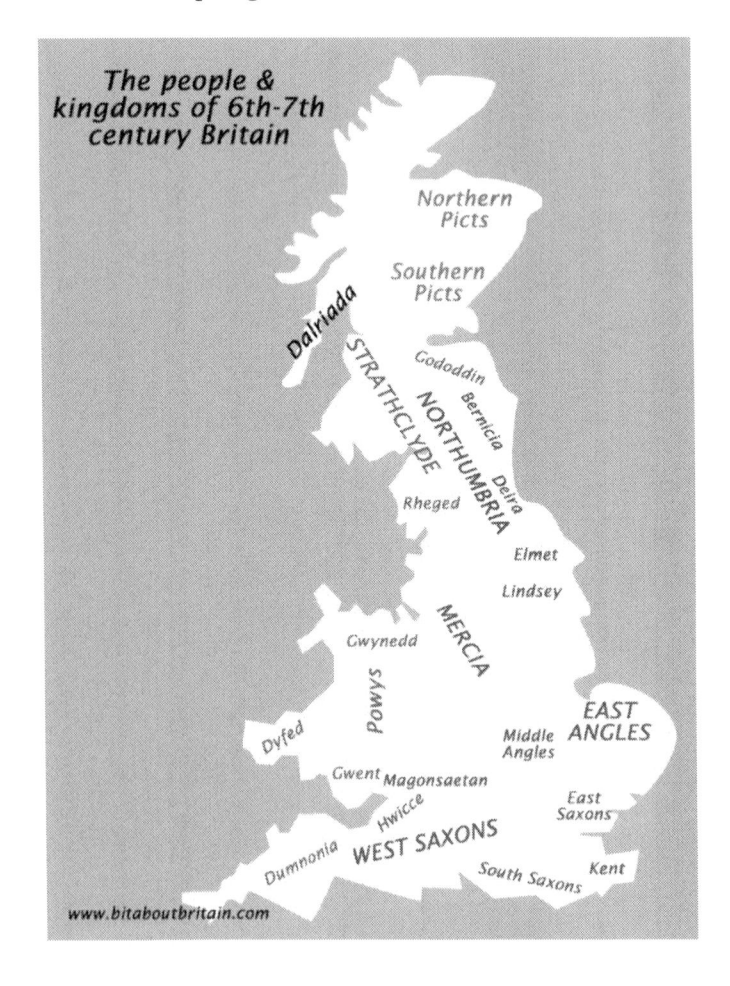

The people & kingdoms of 6th-7th century Britain

Northern Picts
Southern Picts
Dalriada
STRATHCLYDE
Gododdin
Bernicia
NORTHUMBRIA
Deira
Rheged
Elmet
Lindsey
Gwynedd
MERCIA
Powys
Dyfed
Gwent Magonsaetan
Hwicce
Dumnonia WEST SAXONS
Middle Angles
EAST ANGLES
East Saxons
South Saxons
Kent

www.bitaboutbritain.com

Christianity and the age of the saints

How Britain not only became Christian, but also specifically Roman Catholic

Britain, like the rest of Western Europe, has a long Christian heritage. The Church came to wield enormous political and socio-economic power, and religion is such a part of Britain's continuing story, so it is important to understand a bit about how Christianity arrived.

Christianity was born into a Roman world – and would in the end outlive it. The Roman Empire was polytheistic, often chaotically so; in Roman Britain, Graeco-Roman deities tolerantly rubbed shoulders with local spirits, and imports such as the Persian god Mithras. However, the Romans periodically, but not persistently, persecuted Christians. Christianity was revolutionary and challenged the established order; its god ruled on earth as well as in heaven, thus disputing the divinity and authority of emperors; there was suspicion of subversion, of secret rituals and concern – or anger – that Rome's traditions were being denied, thereby incurring the wrath of the true gods.

No one knows exactly when traders or soldiers first brought Christianity to Britain's shores, but it could have been as early as the 1st or 2nd centuries. There was definitely a Christian community in Britain by the early 3rd century. St Alban, generally claimed to be Britain's first Christian martyr, was possibly executed by the Romans in the early 3rd century – maybe the 4th – with a church subsequently being built over his grave. The Edict of Milan, issued under Emperor Constantine in 313 AD, gave Christians freedom of worship and it is known that British bishops attended the Synod (assembly) of Arles in 314 AD. By the end of the 4th century, Christianity was the official religion of the Roman state. There is significant archaeological evidence of Christianity in later Roman

Britain, but the extent of the religion is not known and it probably did not long endure the incursions of the unbelieving Anglo-Saxons. However, in the unconquered western parts of the island, such as Wales and Cornwall, Christianity not only survived the end of Roman rule but also, it is believed, thrived.

The 5th and 6th centuries are sometimes referred to in Wales, as 'the age of the saints' – though the term could be applied more widely across Britain in the 7th century too. Perhaps the best-known figures initially are St Patrick, St David and St Columba. Patrick was a native Briton who lived in the late 4th - early 5th centuries, was captured by pirates and taken to Ireland, where he is reputed to have converted the inhabitants to Christianity. David, another native, had a saintly mother, St Non, and established a monastery and seat of learning at St Davids in the 6th century. Columba was an Irish monk who founded the monastery on the Isle of Iona in 563 AD and is credited with converting the Scots and Northern Picts. From Iona, Christianity was taken to Northumbria. The founder of the monastery at Lindisfarne in 635 AD, Aidan, was a monk from Iona. Welsh tradition also features many lesser-known evangelising saints, such as Petroc, Dyfrig (Dubricus), Illtud, Teilo, Padarn and Deiniol, all journeying the seaways between Brittany, Cornwall, Wales and Ireland, spreading the Word. It was an uplifting time to be a Christian - but hard facts are in short supply. The legendary St Ninian, for example, is said to have landed in the Isle of Whithorn in south-east Scotland to preach to the southern Picts in 397 AD – almost two centuries before Columba established Iona and when Roman rule still prevailed further south. Frankly, we are unlikely to ever know for certain who did what, when, or where.

In any event, these Christian survivors in Britain were Celts, or Romano-British, who evolved their own customs in isolation from the other, arguably more mainstream, branches of Christianity that had developed around the ancient civilisations of the Mediterranean, in Greece, Egypt – and Rome. It was the Roman brand of Christianity that was reintroduced into the southern end of the land that became England, and which ultimately prevailed across the British Isles for the best part of 900 years until the Reformation of the 16th century. The legendary story of how this came about goes that Pope Gregory spotted some fair-haired youngsters in Rome's slave market and asked who they were. "Angles", came the reply. "They are not Angles, but angels", quipped the Pope, and dispatched one of his best men, Augustine, to bring the pagan Anglo-Saxons into the Christian fold. St Augustine landed on the Isle of Thanet, in the Kingdom of Kent, in 597 AD. The King of Kent, Ethelberht, was a pagan, but his wife, Bertha, was daughter of a Frankish king and a Christian – and that must have helped Augustine no end. Even so, Ethelberht insisted on meeting the Christian missionaries in the open, just in case they decided to try their dodgy magic on him. As it happened, Augustine was given permission to preach, managed to convert the king within a year and went on to become the first Archbishop of Canterbury.

Augustine was less successful in establishing authority over native Christians, as the Pope had instructed. Unlike the Roman Catholic Church, the Celtic Church was not an organised, unified, entity – it was more of a monastic tradition and they did things differently from their more recently arrived brethren. The monks even had different hairstyles – the Roman tonsure was the relatively familiar shaved round patch on the top of the head, whereas the Celtic tonsure ran from ear to ear at the front, leaving the hair long at the back. Rather more fundamentally, however, the two sects disagreed over how to calculate the moveable date of Easter, the most significant event and festival in the Christian calendar. It might not have helped Augustine's cause with the Britons that he was probably perceived to be sponsored by an Anglo-Saxon. For some time, representatives of both Roman and Celtic parties worked across the land to replace the worship of Thor, Woden, and others, with Christ; it took time and was not without setbacks. Keen students of this period will encounter a bewildering array of enthusiastic saints and clerics popping in and out of the story. To mention but a few: Paulinus (Roman party), the first Bishop of York; Cedd (Celtic party), missionary to the Kingdom of Mercia and converter of the East Saxons; Mungo (or Kentigern), founder of Glasgow; Cuthbert (Celtic), prior of Melrose and then Lindisfarne, who was largely responsible for the spread of Christianity in the North of England.

The debate about Easter came to a head at the Synod of Whitby in 663 AD (664 in some accounts). The King of Northumbria, Osuiu (or Oswy) was a committed Christian of the Celtic tradition. His wife Eanfled, however, had been brought up in Kent and followed the Roman way. This meant that they sometimes celebrated Easter twice (imagine all that chocolate!). Clearly, something had to be done. And Whitby was the place to do it, because here was Northumbria's principle church and minster, founded in 657 AD by a remarkable lady, Hild, of the Celt party. So the two sides, the Celtic and Roman, came together to sort things out. Bishop Colman of Lindisfarne spoke for the Celts. The Roman case was then put by Wilfred, Abbot of Ripon (later St Wilfred), who concluded by saying that the Roman church received its authority from St Peter, holder of the keys to the kingdom of heaven. The Celts had no answer to that and Osuiu found the argument pretty convincing, observing that if he did not obey the commands of the guardian of the gates of heaven, he might have some difficulty getting in when his time came. Ultimately, the Synod of Whitby determined which brand of Christianity ruled, not just when Easter would fall. And so it came to pass that the Roman Church gained ascendancy over all others in the land, an authority that lasted until Henry VIII wanted a divorce in the 1530s.

In reality, it would take many more years after Whitby before the supremacy of Rome – and indeed, Christianity itself - was accepted throughout Britain. The key figure in laying the foundations for this was Theodore of Tarsus (in modern Turkey), appointed Archbishop of Canterbury by the Pope in 668, who set about organising a centralised church, with clear lines of authority that crossed the boundaries of Britain's various kingdoms. Then, just when things appeared to be going so well, in the late 8th century, along came the Vikings.

Newsflash – Vikings murder defenceless monks

Viking heritage is embedded in parts of Britain

""Dreadful fore-warnings over the land of the Northumbrians, terrifying the people most woefully: these were immense sheets of light rushing through the air, and whirlwinds, and fiery dragons flying across the firmament. These tremendous tokens were soon followed by a great famine: and not long after, on the sixth day before the ides of January in the same year, the harrowing inroads of heathen men made lamentable havoc in the church of God in Holy-island, by rapine and slaughter." – from the Anglo-Saxon Chronicle 793 AD

Like the Saxons, the Vikings – Norsemen from what is now modern Sweden, Norway and Denmark – initially came as raiders. But, also like the Saxons, recognising what a jolly fine place Britain was, many of them wanted to settle down and grow pigs and so forth. Some people think the Vikings have been victims of an unfair Christian-biased press and that they were, deep down, really nice, fun-loving, guys who were just a wee bit misunderstood. In any event, they were astonishingly successful seafarers and global traders, whose impact on history was felt way beyond the British Isles. Vikings established cities and trading centres as far apart as Ireland and Russia, and got to America about 500 years before Columbus did. But they also wanted land. It is ironic that the Anglo-Saxons, once terrible land-hungry invaders themselves, had to deal with a similar problem to the one they had themselves presented to post-Roman Britain. By the way, it is unlikely that Vikings wore horned helmets into battle.

The first recorded Viking raid on Britain was on the Dorset coast in 789 AD and raids continued haphazardly for the next fifty years or so, often on undefended monasteries where the attackers could be sure of little resistance and good plunder. In addition to the famous raid on Lindisfarne, Iona was attacked in 795, 802 and again in 806 when 68 monks were killed. In 835, a major assault was launched against the Isle of Sheppey in southern England and, thereafter, raids of varying scale became pretty much seasonal summer events, along the coast from Cornwall to Kent.

Eventually, some of the raiders took to wintering in Britain and setting their sights on more permanent living arrangements. In 865, the Danes landed what contemporaries called 'the Great Army' in East Anglia, popularly believed to have been led by three sons of the legendary (or mythical) Ragnar Lothbrok, aka Ragnar Hairy-Breeks. The brothers, Ivarr the Boneless, Halfdan and Ubba, wintered in East Anglia and, the following year, struck north and captured York. In 867, they thrashed a Northumbrian army and then proceeded south into the kingdom of Mercia, where they established winter quarters at Nottingham. Here, they were confronted by a joint Mercian-Wessex force, but no major engagement ensued and, the following year, the invaders returned to York. In 869, they headed back to East Anglia, set up camp at Thetford and defeated the East Anglians, led by king – later saint – Edmund near Hoxne in Suffolk. Edmund, tradition has it, was bound to a tree, shot full of arrows, then beheaded.

Probably coincidentally, in 866, western Scotland came under attack by a large Viking army led by Olaf the White, the Norse King of Dublin. In 870, after a four-month siege, the great British fortress of Dumbarton fell. The plunder and number of slaves seized was said to be so great that the victors needed a fleet of 200 longships in which to carry off their booty.

The great Danish army, meanwhile, made their first

incursion into the kingdom of Wessex, basing themselves at Reading. Despite a victory at the Battle of Ashdown in 871, however, Wessex was on the back foot and the new king, Alfred, was forced to buy the Danes off. The Danes subsequently turned their attentions on destroying Mercia. Some also began to settle into permanent homes, particularly around the area that is now modern Yorkshire. By 875, the Danish army had divided into two and one half was ready to threaten Wessex again. Intermittent warfare ensued until, in January 878, a surprise attack was made on Alfred at Chippenham, Wiltshire, where he had been celebrating the Christmas Feast.

Alfred, king of the last remaining Anglo-Saxon kingdom, was forced into hiding in the marshes of Somerset, in Athelney, but was able to gather an army and defeat the Danes later that same year, at Edington (*Ethandune* or *Ethandun*), in Wiltshire. The Danish leader, Guthrum, was even persuaded to become a Christian and change his name to the (apparently) more acceptable Athelstan. Alfred was not powerful enough to expel the Danes entirely, though. England was divided, with the Saxons controlling the south and most of the south-west midlands, and the Danes ruling East Anglia and the north. The influence of this 'Danelaw' can be seen today in language and about 1500 place names – for example anywhere ending in '-*by*' - Derby, Grimsby, Formby - is of Danish origin. (The suffix 'by' denotes a 'farmstead', 'village', or a settlement of some sort). Other common Danish or Norse suffixes in place names are '*thorpe*' (dependent, outlying, settlement), '*holme*' (island, raised ground surrounded by marsh), and '*thwaite*' (clearing, meadow). York, which the Saxons knew as Eoferwic and the Danes called Jorvik, became a key Viking trading centre. In fact, the Vikings profoundly transformed the social, racial and linguistic characteristics of northern England.

Alfred built a defensive network of towns, or fortresses,

called burghs, or burhs, to resist further incursions into Wessex. It was a successful strategy. An Anglo-Saxon document from the 10th century, known as the Burghal Hidage, lists 30 fortified places (burghs), most of which have survived as towns today.

At the time of Alfred's death in 899, Wessex was the one remaining independent English kingdom. Without Alfred, there would have been no England and he is the only English king to be called 'great'. In addition to his military success, he was an excellent law-maker and administrator, is often credited as being the father of the Royal Navy and encouraged reading and writing, both in Latin and Anglo-Saxon (old English). He is also reputed to have been immensely pious and was undoubtedly a first-class propagandist. Further, he is said to have suffered from Crohn's Disease. There is a grand statue of Alfred in Winchester, the old capital of Wessex, and you'd never know he wasn't well from that…

The situation in Wales and what is now Scotland at this time was pretty confusing. The west of Britain was prone to attacks by Irish raiders as well as by Norse Vikings. The latter settled in parts of the north, particularly the north and east of Scotland. Slavery was rife – and it really is about time someone apologised for that, don't you think? But neither the Saxons nor the Vikings ever conquered Wales. It's even likely that some Britons from Wales may have fought alongside their erstwhile enemies, the Saxons, against the common foe.

The Anglo-Saxons clashed with the Celtic kingdoms of Dalriada and Strathclyde in the south and west of Scotland, and with the Picts – by whom they were roundly defeated – but made no permanent penetration beyond the borders (which came to be part of the Anglo-Saxon kingdom of Northumbria). The Picts ruled much of the north and the Highlands, but were progressively weakened by the Viking coastal raids that threatened the whole of the British Isles.

Gradually, the Picts came more under the influence of the *Scotii* of Dalriada (traditionally thought to be originally from Ireland), in the west of modern Scotland. In 843 AD, Kenneth MacAlpin (*Cináed mac Ailpín*) a Gaelic or Pictish warlord, united the people of Dalriada with the people of Pictland against a common foe, the Viking Norsemen. Kenneth MacAlpin's descendents became kings of Scotland. The Vikings had not only been raiding, but also using parts of Scotland as bases and in 875 the northern isles of Shetland and Orkney fell under Harald Fair Hair, King of Norway.

Why London is the capital of Britain

People talk of a north-south divide in Britain, but it was once even more serious than it is now

It's all a matter of power and geography, and t'was ever thus. In the 9th century, the Danes defeated the old Anglo-Saxon kingdoms of Northumbria, East Anglia and Mercia. If the Danes had beaten Alfred of Wessex too, maybe the capital of Britain would have been York. Or Copenhagen. Without Alfred, there would not only have been no England but, also, no English-speaking world. Alfred's power-base was manifestly in the south of England and by the time he died the components of an organised, unified, state were pretty much in place.

London was also the largest trading settlement in the whole of Britain. The original Saxon invaders, suspicious of urban areas, had for the most part ignored the old Roman town, underneath the present City of London, but by the 8th century had developed an important cosmopolitan trading centre, *Lundenwic*, immediately to the west of it. It offered a sheltered anchorage, handy for the European mainland, and its position as a crossing point over the barrier of the River Thames at London Bridge also gave it a unique position in north-south communications. The Saxons have left their memory behind in names like *Aldwych* (old town) and *Strand* (beach). The Danes attacked London in 842, again in 851 and by 871 were in occupation. Despite the fact that, technically, Lundenwic was in the Kingdom of Mercia, Alfred thought it vital enough to re-take the city in 886 and secure its fortifications and position outside the area of Danelaw. His son-in-law, Ethelred of Mercia, was charged with maintaining it as a valuable commercial centre under Anglo-Saxon control.

After Alfred's death, his son Edward and daughter Æthelflæd set about wearing down Danish rule south of the

Humber. Alfred's grandson, Æthelstan (Athelstan) took York, defeating the Danes in Northumbria, and in 927 he accepted the submission of the kings of the Scots, Strathclyde Welsh, Cumbria and the Earl of Northumbria at Eamont Bridge, near Penrith in modern-day Cumbria. The southern Anglo-Saxon Æthelstan is known as the first king of all England - *Englaland*, the land of the Angles. But what had been won by conquest was consolidated by laws and regulation - for example with regard to coinage - that applied equally across the whole kingdom. This was no casual toppling of tribal military rivals; it was organised state rule.

However, these were violent times when fortunes ebbed and flowed. In 937, Æthelstan crushed a combined invasion of Norse and Scots at the Battle of Brunanburh. No one knows for certain where the battle took place, but it was possibly somewhere on the Wirral in North West England; other suggested locations include Burnswark in Dumfries and Galloway. Anglo-Saxon control of the north then seems to have collapsed after Æthelstan's death. But, by the reign of Edgar in the 970s, a more united kingdom of England seemed to be once again emerging. Then, the next few years seem to have been plagued by faction-fighting – and more raids by Danes and Norse. In 991 a Viking force sacked Ipswich and defeated the English at Maldon in Essex. In 1002, King Ethelred the Unready ordered the massacre of all Danes in England, including peaceful settlers, and then attempted to buy the invaders off with bribes – known as 'Danegeld'. The massacre, known as the St Brice's Day Massacre, provoked an invasion by King Sweyn Forkbeard of Denmark in 1013 and Ethelred fled into exile in Normandy. Sweyn died in 1014 and Ethelred returned, to spend the rest of his days occupied in warfare against Sweyn's son, Cnut. Ethelred died in 1016, Cnut defeated Ethelred's son, Edmund, at the battle of Ashingdon later that year, shortly after which Edmund died too. So England got a Danish king after all, Cnut, and it was left to him to unify the country once more. One of his first acts in 1017 was to divide the land into four administrative earldoms: Wessex, Mercia, East Anglia and Northumbria – retaining Wessex under his own direct control. The same year, Cnut married Ethelred's widow, Emma of Normandy, who was herself of Norse descent and by all accounts a remarkable woman.

After Cnut's death in 1035 (he was buried in Winchester, capital of the old Saxon Kingdom of Wessex), the throne of the English state returned to the Anglo-Saxon line. The new king, a son of Ethelred and Emma, is known to history as King Edward the Confessor. And one of allegedly pious King Edward's greatest legacies was the decision to build a grand church, upstream of Lundenwic, on swampy ground at the mouth of the River Tyburn – his 'West Minster' – as well as a splendid palace next door. Just as the area by the old Roman City of London was growing in commercial importance, so would Westminster become the centre for royal administration. And this pattern continued; even now, the City enjoys a unique status in the economy of the United Kingdom, while the centre of government is based around Westminster.

Meanwhile, back in 1018 at the battle of Carham on the River Tweed, the King of Scotland, Malcolm II *'Forranach'* (the Destroyer), combined with Owen the Bald, King of Strathclyde, to defeat the Anglo-Saxon Uhtred, Earl of Northumbria. Though Cnut later defeated Malcolm, the battle of Carham appears to have settled the oft-disputed Lothian/Borders area and placed the English/Scots boundary along the River Tweed. By the mid 11th century, the boundaries of England on a map would have looked pretty much as they do today, though it was still a bit fuzzy round the edges and the northern frontier was a little further south in Cumbria than it is now.

Neither Wales nor Scotland was a unified entity at that

time, as we would understand it. Wales consisted of different independent kingdoms, or principalities, though Gwynedd under the leadership of Gruffydd ap Llywelyn was emerging as the most powerful force. What we know as Scotland comprised the Norse Earldom of Orkney (in the north and west), the old Celtic Kingdom of Strathclyde (which included a good chunk of modern-day north west England), as well as the Kingdom of the Scots north of the Forth and covering most of the Highlands.

However, England was just about to be invaded all over again – and that would be another game-changer for everyone.

How the Normans shaped world history

The Normans crushed the Saxons and a hybrid culture evolved that became uniquely British

Britain changed forever on 14 October 1066. In fact, the defeat of the English (Saxons) under King Harold, by the bastard Duke William of Normandy and his invaders at the Battle of Hastings is one of those events that came to have repercussions for the whole world.

Think about it: for one thing, the modern English language wouldn't exist – the President of the USA would probably be talking some form of German...or Spanish...or French. And they may never have 'found' New Zealand (not that its inhabitants realised it was lost). So there would be no All Blacks rugby team. Peter Jackson (if he had existed) would have had to have filmed 'The Lord of the Rings' somewhere else. Without the Normans, J R R Tolkien (whose ancestors came from Germany) would have probably written a different book, and certainly not in English. And so on. You get the point: some things make a huge difference, and the Battle of Hastings certainly did. The date is, rightly, one of the most famous in British history; everyone should remember it, and perhaps also pay a visit to Senlac Field, in Battle, Sussex, to see where the future was so dramatically set in motion.

The background to Hastings is fascinating. In simple terms, there was a difference of opinion as to who should be king of England. Should it be Harold, the son of the leading Saxon Godwinson family, who believed he had been named as successor by the previous king, Edward the Confessor? Or should it be William, who had allegedly been promised the throne by both Harold (in a rash moment) and Edward? Of course, it helped that both men wanted the job so much. Harold, who had no claim on the throne by descent, had himself crowned before old

Edward's body was barely cold. William, seriously disgruntled, set about raising enough men, supplies and ships to invade. His ability to convince folk that Harold had broken a sacred oath that William should be king helped gather considerable support including, significantly, from the Church. Eventually, William raised an invasion fleet of 700 ships.

The Norman invasion in southern England was almost immediately preceded by another in the north led by the King of Norway, Harald Hardrada, and King Harold of England's estranged brother, Tostig. Landing in the Humber in the late summer of 1066, the Norsemen rapidly overcame local Northumbrian earls at the Battle of Fulford, near York. Harold was expecting the Norman invasion and had been hanging around the south coast in anticipation. But William was delayed by storms in the Channel. So when Harold heard about t'trouble up north, he reacted quickly, marched his army 200 miles or so in 5 days, gathering more men en route, and completely surprised the invaders on 25 September at Stamford Bridge, near York (not to be confused with a football ground in Chelsea, further south). The Norsemen were wholly unprepared and many had no time to put on any armour. The English victory was so overwhelming that, of the 300 ships that had formed the invasion force, it is said only 24 were needed to sail the survivors home. Both Harald Hardrada and Tostig were killed in the fighting. Then the news came that William had landed in Sussex, at Pevensey on 28 September, and was ravaging the area – Harold's home turf; so he trudged back south again…

The Saxon army that formed up on top of a commanding ridge on the road from the Sussex coast to London was apparently well-equipped, well organised - and terrifying. *"Ut! Ut! Ut!"*, they screamed the ancient Saxon war cry at the invader, clashing their weapons from their shield wall. Facing them at the bottom of the slope was a mixed army of Normans (originally 'Norsemen'), allies and mercenaries, including Bretons, French and Flems. It has been suggested that the Saxons should have won. What is certain is that it was a long battle that ebbed and flowed one way then another all day. And the Saxons lost. Harold, hit by an arrow in the eye, cut down, or both, was mutilated and his body left for his mistress, Edith Swan-Neck, to identify the following day.

William consolidated his victory in the south and then, avoiding the easily-defended London Bridge, crossed the River Thames further west, at Wallingford. He accepted the surrender of the English leadership at Berkhamsted in December, and on Christmas Day he was crowned King William I at Westminster. This did not mean there was no further opposition. The Normans set about stamping their mark on the country they had conquered, relentlessly spreading their rule ever northward, crushing resistance. In places, the conquest was particularly harsh and barbaric – the 'harrying of the north' (of England) is possibly the best (or worst) example of Norman brutality, where entire villages and their inhabitants were viciously put to fire and sword; some communities simply ceased to exist. The Harrying of the North was William's final solution to eliminating resistance, yet the event is barely mentioned in some history books. A contemporary chronicler, Oderic Vitalis, wrote that 100,000 people perished (the population of England at this time was less than 2 million), and described rotting corpses covered in worms lying along the roadsides with no one to bury them, not a single inhabited village to be seen along the road from York to Durham and the only moving things being packs of wolves and wild dogs feeding on the dead.

All of the people of Britain would, in time, come to be dominated by the Norman French-speaking elite and their descendents. In Wales, meanwhile, one unpopular neighbour was swapped for another; intermittent warfare between the two eventually came to a head 200 years later. The situation was slightly different in Scotland.

The history of Scotland is to some extent the history of the differences between Lowland and Highland. The rulers were based in the lowlands, strongly influenced by their neighbours to the south. Malcolm III of Scotland married Margaret of Wessex, sister to Edgar, the Saxon heir to the English throne, and invaded England in 1070 to show support for his brother-in-law. William returned the favour and secured the homage of the Scottish king at Abernethy – an act that would haunt future kings of Scotland. Under Margaret's sons, ties with the court in England were strengthened through marriage, Norman culture was introduced and powerful Normans gained lands in Scotland. Norman influence in Scotland came not by conquest, but by gradual infiltration. You could say that the Normans helped forge Scotland almost as much as they did England.

Celts, Romans, Anglo-Saxons, Vikings – the Normans were the latest in a long line of invaders that shaped Britain, culturally and politically. The physical legacy of the Normans is perhaps most vividly seen today in the castles and cathedrals they built; they are, quite bluntly, symbols of power. Norman-French aristocracy replaced the defeated Saxons. The Normans introduced trial by jury and feudalism, a system that relied upon a pyramid of supporting dues and privileges, with the king at the peak. William also instigated the Domesday Book, a survey which covered most of England detailing the land, who owned it and its value; it is a unique socio-economic record of the time. Most of the almost 13,500 places noted in it still exist today.

What might be called 'the French Connection', inevitably moved Britain away from northern German/Scandinavian influence. There was less regional autonomy based on the shires. The Saxons survived, but as a kind of under-class – many of the Anglo-Saxon elite had actually fled, some to the Lowlands of Scotland. The Saxon language – old English – survived too, but was influenced by the French of the court and ruling classes. By the 14th century it is possible to see a language that is kind of recognisable as English...

> *"Whan that Aprill with his shoures soote, the droghte of March hath perced to the roote..."* - When in April the sweet showers fall, that pierce March's drought to the root and all..." - From Chaucer's Prologue to the Canterbury Tales.

The Battle of Hastings was one of those milestone events in British history; it was not just a crushing defeat for the Saxon English, but a step toward evolving the hybrid culture that is uniquely British.

3 LATER MEDIEVAL BRITAIN

Brits invent parliamentary democracy

The medieval roots of modern British government

Most people know that the ancient Greeks invented democracy (*demos* – 'the people' + *kratia* – 'power'). But we Brits like to imagine it was us – Westminster is 'the mother of parliaments', and all that. In fact, Iceland's *Althing* and Sweden's *Jamtamot* date back to the 10th century, both much older than the Westminster Parliament, and the Isle of Man's *Tynwald* also claims a 1,000-year history. Possibly, the UK's Parliament has had better publicity. In any event, parliamentary democracy, for all its shortcomings, has had a profound impact on the making of Britain: how did it start?

You'd think that medieval kings could do pretty much as they liked. It certainly wasn't a good idea to upset one. But it stands to reason that all monarchs need sufficient cash and support in order to wield power. Saxon kings had ruled largely through the *Witenagemot*, or *Witan,* an assembly or counsel of nobles. Post Norman Conquest Kings called 'Great Councils' (the forerunner of parliaments – a word derived from the old French *parlement* – 'speaking'), but they had to deal with the realities of feudalism. From the King of England's point of view, one of the flaws of feudalism was that it depended entirely on the support of very powerful subjects indeed (like barons and bishops), many of whom had significant economic and military assets. Therefore a good chunk of British history chronicles the inevitable struggle between monarchs who wanted to do things that their rich and influential friends and associates did not want them to.

So, let's mention King John. History paints John, who ruled 1199-1216, as a rather unlikable figure, definitely not as cuddly as other monarchs. He certainly hacked off the Pope – which could be an awkward thing to do in those days. Legend has it that Robin Hood didn't like him much either. His unpleasantness included playing fast and loose with other men's daughters and wives. But a more lasting legacy was the fact that he very carelessly managed to lose most of the family lands in France. His father, Henry II, had been one of the most powerful rulers in Europe, governing territories that included Normandy, Maine, Brittany, Anjou, Touraine, Aquitaine, Gascony and Toulouse – lands collectively known as the 'Angevin Empire'. Under John, all of these lands were lost to the King of France with the exception of part of Aquitaine and Gascony. John's attempts to raise more and more taxes to fund unsuccessful military campaigns to recover these lost assets proved to be the last straw. In 1215 the leading nobles forced John to sign the *Magna Carta*, or 'Great Charter', at Runneymede on the River Thames. Magna Carta shouldn't be seen as some sort of Bill of Rights, as some people suggest – and it was largely ignored anyway – but it is enormously symbolic, and significant in stating that the monarch is not above the law. Magna Carta laid the foundation for future governance. There are 63 clauses, the most significant of which is No 39, which states:

"No free man shall be seized or imprisoned, or stripped of his rights or possessions, or deprived of his standing in any other way, nor will we proceed with force against him, or send others to do so, except by the lawful judgement of his equals or by the law of the land."

Clause 40 reassuringly goes on:

"To no one will we sell, to no one deny or delay right or justice."

This is pretty noble and uncompromising stuff – these are two of the four clauses that remain part of English Law and, often, the ones that people get most excited about. In 1215, of course, there were not that many free men (or women) in England. But these words unequivocally say that the law is not subject to the whim of one person and that all of us are equal and accountable under it. The charter also includes an early version of 'no taxation without representation' and establishes a principle that certain rights could be settled by a council of 25 barons.

John's son, Henry III (ruled 1216-72), was clearly a chip off the old block. Some of the great and the good felt they were being ignored, they didn't like some of Henry's friends and he supported an invasion of Sicily without telling them. So the barons forced Henry to form a council and call more regular parlements. Eventually, war broke out between the King's supporters on the one hand and a rebel faction on the other, under Simon de Montfort, the Earl of Leicester. The King was defeated and captured at the Battle of Lewes in 1264 and de Montfort called a parliament which for the first time included representatives from each shire and borough. Simon de Montfort's parliament of January 1265 is seen by many as a precursor to the House of Commons, and unquestionably future English monarchs would be forced to deal with Parliament; though de Montfort almost certainly never envisaged the parliamentary democracy we all aspire to today.

Henry's son Edward I, who ruled from 1272-1307, was a more wily authoritarian than his father. He also had an agenda to unite Britain under his rule. So he used parliament often, primarily to raise money for his wars against the French, Scots and Welsh. And it is really from the reign of Edward that the English Parliament began to be an integral, but initially irregular, part of English governance, particularly after Edward's so-called 'Model Parliament' of 1295. This included representatives of the lower clergy for the first time, as well as two knights from each county and two burgesses (officials) from each city, town or borough. Thus was set the format, or 'model' for most future parliaments which consisted of three institutions - the Commons, the Lords and the Monarch.

Whilst the Monarch sought to obtain Parliament's approval for money-raising taxes, it then became normal for Parliament to seek something in return, a *quid pro quo*. This eventually resulted in Parliament presenting and debating petitions, or 'bills', (from *bille*, in turn derived from the Medieval Latin *bulla*, seal, sealed document) requiring the monarch's assent – and therefore developing Parliament's legislative authority.

The medieval Parliament met in the old Palace of Westminster, which burned down in 1834, or in the Chapter House or Refectory of Westminster Abbey. From 1547, it had the use of the Palace's chapel. Under Henry VIII, Parliament underwent a fundamental change. Henry's break with Rome in the 16th century transferred all religious authority to the Crown and, under Henry's direction, Parliament found its breadth of interests and power dramatically increased – no aspect of government was beyond its legislative remit. Thus Parliament took on religious, social and economic matters.

Though Parliament still existed only by the monarch's will, it is inevitable that the relationship between an absolutist monarch and a parliament will be an uneasy one. In order to get his/her way, the monarch has to be able to control parliament. Parliament, on the other hand, might feel it should control the purse strings and limit the monarch's power. In the 17th century, under King Charles I, the relationship irretrievably broke down and Parliament became a revolutionary body. The debate was eventually resolved by war – a classic example of the continuation of politics by other means.

A Bit About Britain's History

How Scotland was born

Scotland manages to create itself – with a little help from the King of England

In the 9th century, Kenneth MacAlpin (*Cináed mac Ailpín*) merged Dalriada or *Dál Riata*, the Kingdom of the Scotii, with the Kingdom of the Picts. This new kingdom, known as Alba, would eventually morph into Scotland. Kenneth MacAlpin is traditionally credited with being the first King of the Scots, but Scotland lay in the future and Alba was many years from being a unified state with defined borders. MacAlpin's successors battled internal as well as external foes just to secure their positions, and few of them died peacefully in their beds. By the end of the 10th century, the Scots controlled Strathclyde and Lothian. By the 11th century, squabbles, first with the Earls of Northumberland and then with the Kings of England, frequently saw the King of Scotland coming off worse. During the reign of Malcolm III, from 1058 to 1093, the court and clergy were dramatically Anglicised under the influence of the King's second wife, Queen Margaret, an Anglo-Saxon princess raised at the court of Edward the Confessor. By the 12th and 13th centuries, marriage and the introduction of the feudal system meant that lowland Scotland was very much part of the Norman world. Many Scottish nobles had Norman blood and some (including the King of the Scots) had lands in England. The French-speaking elite squabbled amongst themselves and theoretically ruled over a population that spoke Scots in the Lowlands and Gaelic in the Highlands. Government of the Highlands, however, still relied on kinship, where the rule of the clan chiefs – effectively tribal leaders - was supreme. The Western Isles, Orkneys and Shetland were ruled by the King of Norway until the 13th century. The Scots held the Norwegians off at the Battle of Largs (nice little town on the west coast, good ice-cream parlour) in 1263 and, three years later, the Western Isles (and the Isle of Man) became Scottish. However, an absence of unity and common purpose among Scottish leaders was often a stumbling-block in the creation of a nation state.

Having a large and powerful neighbour to the south was both a temptation and a threat. In theory, the boundaries between England and Scotland had been settled in 1237 by the Treaty of York, though this did not stop both sides raiding each other's border areas. But the stakes were raised, far beyond a bit of sheep stealing, by Edward I of England – because he aspired to a unified island of Britain which, naturally, would be ruled by the King of England. You could argue that Edward was the father of Scottish (and possibly Welsh) nationalism; perhaps, if he'd acted differently, common ground would have resulted in some form of union 400 years sooner, and saved a lot of unnecessary hassle – and bloodshed. As it is, Edward is known to history as 'the Hammer of the Scots'.

The sudden accidental death of King Alexander III in 1286 meant that the heir to the Scottish throne became his infant granddaughter, Margaret, both of Alexander's sons having predeceased him. Edward, keeping a sharp eye on affairs, was keen to engage his son (the future Edward II) to the young heiress, which would have joined the two kingdoms by marriage. But Edward's plans were upset when Margaret, known to history as 'the Maid of Norway' (because she was the daughter of the King of Norway), died in Orkney on her way to Scotland in 1290 at the age of seven. This put the Scots nobility into a bit of a fankle: who should rule? It boiled down to two main contenders – Robert Bruce of Annandale, grandfather of the more famous Robert the Bruce, and John Balliol, whose father was founder of Balliol College, Oxford. Both Bruce and Balliol were aristocratic Normans, incidentally. The Scots asked Edward, as the most powerful lord in Britain, to arbitrate; and, in 1292, he chose Balliol.

Some say that Balliol was a mere puppet of Edward's – he is sometimes known derisively as the 'Toom Tabard' - empty coat. But when Edward made it clear that he expected Scottish support for his wars in France (he was a busy chap, was Edward), Balliol allied himself with the French. Furious, Edward invaded in 1296, massacred the inhabitants of Berwick upon Tweed (at that time an important Scottish port), decisively defeated Balliol in battle at Dunbar, took him prisoner and, for good measure, pinched the Stone of Destiny on which the Kings of the Scots had been traditionally crowned. There was no King of Scotland, the Scottish nobility paid homage to Edward and the Scots were for all practical purposes under English rule. The Stone of Destiny was finally returned 700 years later, in 1996.

A rebellion began in 1297, led by the legendary William Wallace (or Mel Gibson). Probably the son of a minor landowner, Wallace came to prominence by leading a successful attack on Lanark, killing the English sheriff, Sir William Heselrig, in the process. The story goes that Heselrig had murdered Wallace's wife and that Wallace retaliated by the ghastly dismembering of Heselrig's corpse. He went on to wage a successful guerrilla war against the English, culminating in the defeat of a considerably larger English army at Stirling Bridge in September 1297, in partnership with Andrew de Moray (Andy Murray). De Moray was mortally wounded, but Wallace was knighted, allegedly by Robert the Bruce, and made one of the Guardians of the Kingdom of Scotland. More triumphant hit and run tactics followed, but in July 1298 the Scots were heavily beaten at the Battle of Falkirk. Wallace went abroad to plead Scotland's cause, returning in 1303. In August 1305, he was betrayed, captured by the Scottish knight Sir John de Menteith at Robroystoun near Glasgow, taken to London and put on trial for treason. Wallace denied the charge, pointing out – reasonably, but possibly naively - that he had never sworn allegiance to the English King so how could he be a traitor? Inevitably, he was deemed guilty and hanged, drawn and quartered at Smithfield. A memorial stands near the spot today.

The Bruce (de Bruis) family had supported Edward's invasion of 1296. But young Robert the Bruce allied himself to Wallace and, murdering his adversary John Comyn along the way, managed to get himself crowned King of Scotland in 1306. Death near Carlisle thwarted Edward's personal ambitions (well it would, wouldn't it?) and the metaphorical hammer passed to his somewhat disengaged and allegedly damp son, Edward II. For years, Bruce fought a guerrilla campaign against the English, and other Scots, gradually building his power base until Edward II couldn't ignore him any longer. A massive English army was assembled to relieve the garrison at Stirling Castle, which Bruce's brother (another Edward) had under siege. In the shadow of the castle, close to the Bannock Burn, Robert the Bruce's force roundly defeated the much larger English army over the 23 and 24 June 1314. Rumour has it that the English didn't stop running until they got to Dunbar, 60 miles away.

Bannockburn effectively sealed Scottish independence, but Bruce drove the point home with a series of brutal raids into northern England. Scottish independence was recognised by the Pope in 1324 through the Declaration of Arbroath (1320) and by the new English King Edward III under the Treaty of Northampton in 1328. Subsequently, Edward III decided he'd signed the treaty under duress and invaded Scotland in 1333. But, despite that, and although the Scots and English were frequently at odds over the centuries, the fact is that, under Bruce, Scotland became "separate in all things from the Kingdom of England." And it stayed that way until a Scottish King became King of England in 1603. That king, James Stuart, was Bruce's direct descendant. Bruce's daughter, Marjorie, married Walter, 6th Lord Steward of Scotland and their son was the first Stuart King of Scotland, Robert II, who reigned from 1371-1390. The name 'Stewart' or 'Stuart' is derived from 'Steward'.

Whatever happened to Wales?

Wales is conquered and becomes an English colony

Wales, like Scotland, was not a unified political entity in the early Middle Ages. It consisted of a number of independent kingdoms, the largest of which were Gwynedd in the north west, Deheubarth in the south west and Powys in between the two. Its kings and chieftains variously fought each other and whoever happened to be running England. The Normans seized territory where they could, but didn't have it all their own way; in 1136, the Welsh crushingly defeated a Norman army at Crug Mawr, near Cardigan.

Along the lands between England and Wales, straddling the old 8th century Mercian boundary of Offa's Dyke, ruled the Marcher Lords. With principal bases in Chester, Shrewsbury and Hereford, the Marcher Lords were first appointed by William the Conqueror, who gave them enormous powers to do virtually what they liked. So they did. Among other things, they built a large number of castles, and the area remains today a veritable feast for any castle-lover.

One native leader emerged from the internal struggles and wars in the Welsh heartlands. Llywelyn ab Iorwerth of Gwynedd (also known as Llywelyn *Fawr* 'the Great') made himself effective ruler of the whole of Wales by the time he died in 1240. More domestic strife and bloodshed followed Llwelyn's passing until his grandson, Llywelyn ap Gruffydd, proclaimed himself Prince of Wales in 1258 – a title that was actually recognised by King Henry III of England in 1267. Then along came our dear friend, Edward I who, naturally, had other ideas…Edward demanded homage from Llywelyn, who refused; repeatedly.

The inevitable war that ensued in 1277 culminated in Llywelyn being tricked into a meeting in Builth Wells in 1282 and killed. Dafydd, his brother, was captured the following year and hanged, drawn and quartered in Shrewsbury. Thus ended Wales's very brief period of unified independence. And so the last of the Celts who had occupied these lands since before Roman times were finally overcome. From this point on, England ran Wales more or less like a colony for the next 250 years or so.

Edward reinforced English domination through a network of impressive castles – which are still imposing, even today. In 1301, he generously decided to give Wales their own prince again - his eldest son, Edward, became the first (English) Prince of Wales. I bet that brought a welcome in the valleys.

Despite this, Welsh culture continued to flourish – as it does still, of course. There were a number of rebellions after Edward's conquest, the most notable of which was probably that of Owain Glyndwr in 1400. By 1403, Glyndwr, in allegiance with two powerful English nobles, Sir Edmund Mortimer and the Earl of Northumberland, had become a serious threat to English rule and the King, Henry IV (both parts). With further support from England's old enemy, the French, he even succeeded in controlling much of West Wales and holding his own courts. But, bit by bit, Glyndwr's power was beaten away and he was reduced to becoming a guerrilla leader hiding in the mountains. By 1413, he had disappeared; no one knows what happened to him. And no further attempt was ever made to forcibly gain Welsh independence.

Later Medieval Britain

Why France isn't part of Britain

Problems with close neighbours

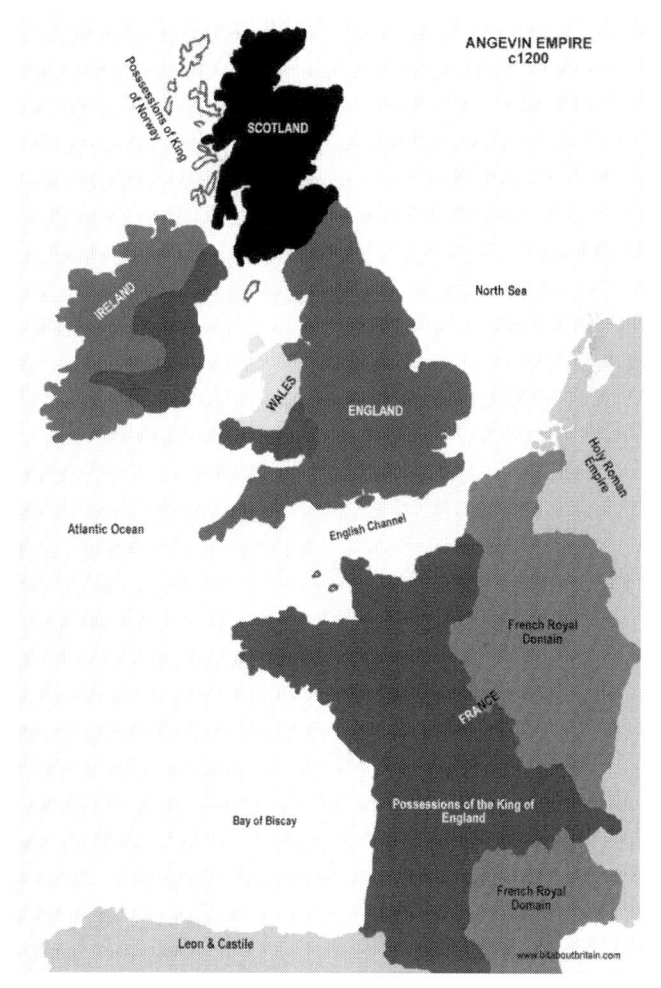

You may have noticed that France isn't part of Britain. But at one time, through inheritance, marriage or conquest, the Kings of England ruled enormous chunks of what is now France, as well as lands in Wales and Ireland. The French Connection all began when Duke William of Normandy became King William I of England in 1066. Under his great-grandson, Henry II (1133-1189), the so-called 'Angevin Empire' stretched from Scotland to the Pyrenees and included Normandy, Maine, Brittany, Anjou, Touraine, Aquitaine, Gascony and Toulouse. 'Angevin' refers to the House of Anjou, members of which were kings of England.

Neighbours sometimes fall out (one of ours occasionally causes no end of trouble) and by the 14th century, the King of England's lands across the Channel had been reduced to just Gascony. In 1337, King Philip VI of France seized parts of Gascony, which belonged to the English crown by inheritance. Edward III of England, who was also irritated by French support for Scottish raids and piracy against English ships, responded by pressing his own claim to the throne of France – which some argued was better than Philip's (Philip was cousin to the previous king, Charles IV, and Edward was Charles' nephew on his mother's side – but French law did not accept succession through the female line). Thus began what history knows as 'The Hundred Years War' – which actually spanned 116 years.

So Edward invaded France in 1346, winning a resounding victory against superior odds at the Battle of Crécy. Crécy is considered a military milestone because the French cavalry was overwhelmed by English and Welsh archers; nobility was defeated by a largely peasant army that fought on foot. One of France's allies at the battle was blind King John of Bohemia who, possibly unsurprisingly, was slain during the fighting. Legend has it that the 16 year old Prince of Wales, Edward of Woodstock, was so moved by this sacrifice that he plucked the dead king's three ostrich feathers from the battlefield and adopted them and the motto, *Ich dien* ('I serve') as his heraldic device. The legend is somewhat dodgy, but it's a good story and the badge of the Prince of Wales – three white ostrich feathers on a black background - definitely dates from this time. This particular Prince of Wales is also known to history as 'the Black Prince', possibly because he wore black armour; or, some say, because he allegedly had a brutal temper and reputation, which included the (disputed) slaughter of 3,000 citizens of Limoges.

After Crécy, King Edward laid siege to Calais for eleven months. At the end of this, the townsfolk were starving and another story can be added to the annals of Anglo-French history. It goes that six burghers (officials) came to Edward, offering their lives if he would spare their fellow citizens. The King's wife, Philippa of Hainault (an area in what is now northern France, southern Belgium), pleaded for the men's lives and the King graciously gave in. Anyway, Calais was taken and remained English for the next 200 years.

The Prince of Wales, Edward of Woodstock (he was never known as the Black Prince in his lifetime), invaded France again in 1356, winning another famous victory that year at the Battle of Poitiers. During the battle, the French King, John II, was taken prisoner and subsequently held captive in the Tower of London, as well as in the sumptuous Savoy Palace – which used to stand on the site of the famous hotel on London's Strand. The French King joined the King of Scotland, David II, in captivity. (David had been captured by the English at the Battle of Neville's Cross, near Durham, in 1346.) Eventually, an enormous ransom was settled for John's return to France – although he died before he could be released – and both sides agreed territorial concessions. However, in 1369, the French got a new, vigorous, king, Charles V. The English were driven back and the French threatened the English coast - for example, attacking Portsmouth in 1369, 1377 and 1380.

French resurgence actually resulted in a period of relative calm in Anglo-French affairs. Edward III was ill and died in 1377. His heir, Edward of Woodstock, had died in 1376, leaving the throne of England to the King's ten year old grandson, Richard II. The young King Richard had to contend with revolting peasants (the Peasants' Revolt of 1381) and, eventually, being overthrown by his cousin, Henry Bolingbroke, who became Henry IV and probably had poor Richard starved to death in Pontefract Castle. Henry, in turn, was also preoccupied with rebellion at home and war in Wales and it was his son, Prince Hal, who as Henry V decided to revisit the English King's claim to the throne of France.

Henry V set sail for France in August 1415 with an army of about 10,000 men. Incidentally, this venture was partly financed by one Richard (Dick) Whittington – not a pantomime figure, but an actual person who really was mayor of London. Anyway, landing in Normandy, Henry laid siege to Harfleur, which surrendered after about a month. His forces depleted by illness, Henry was forced to abandon a planned march on Paris and instead headed north to Calais. He found his way barred near the village of Azincourt by a French army which outnumbered the by now very hungry English by about four to one. However, though estimates of precise numbers vary considerably, the Battle of Agincourt on 25 October 1415 was another triumphant victory for the English. It is said that the cream of French nobility perished in the bloody mud of Agincourt – and, controversially, many prisoners were also murdered on Henry's orders. Supported by the Duke of Burgundy, Henry went on to reconquer Normandy. Finally, the French gave in. In 1420, the Treaty of Troyes agreed that Henry's heirs would be kings of France and, to seal the deal, he married Catherine of Valois, daughter of the French King, Charles the Mad.

But in 1422 Henry died of dysentery (after ten years on

the throne), leaving the kingdom of England in the care of regents for his 9-month old son, Henry VI. In 1429, events turned again. Joan of Arc, allegedly motivated by visions from God to drive out 'les Roastbeefs', began the French recovery by inspiring the recapture of Orléans. She was later burnt at the stake by the English. Despite Henry VI being crowned King of France at Notre-Dame in 1431, the French gradually regained most of the captured territory. Maine and Anjou were handed over as part of the Treaty of Tours, an agreement for a 20-year peace which included young Henry's marriage to Margaret of Anjou in 1445. That peace was soon broken and the decisive French victory at Castillon in 1453 is generally thought to mark the final end of the war. The English still had Calais, but the loss of territory was hugely unpopular and is often cited as one of the reasons for dissatisfaction with the reign of Henry VI and the Lancastrian party, leading to the terrible English civil war, the Wars of the Roses.

The battles of the Hundred Years War were dominated by the fearsome English (and Welsh) terror weapon, the longbow, and by the emerging use of cannon. Whether England could ever have won the war is doubtful; its armies operated far from home, with long supply-lines, often in hostile territory and were habitually decimated by hunger and disease – notably, dysentery. At times, English soldiers were reduced to violent banditry.

Essentially, the Hundred Years War was an inter-dynastic conflict over who ruled in France, which had been off and on since 1066 and which the King of France ultimately won. King Edward III of England was as much French as English, and French was still the official language of the law in England at the time. Many modern legal terms – for example 'attorney', 'bailiff' and 'defendant' – are derived from French. Though 'nations' did not exist in the way we understand them, the Hundred Years War did help develop separate national identities on both sides of the

Channel. Henry V was actually the first King of England to communicate primarily in English, the language of his people.

As a footnote, the English monarch's claim to the French throne was only given up in 1801.

When death walked the land

The only defence was to run away – if you could

The 'Black Death' or 'Great Pestilence' swept through Europe between around 1346–1353, where it eventually killed between 30-60% of the population – maybe 25 million people, though some historians estimate twice that figure. The disease originated 'somewhere in the east' and arrived in southern or south western England in the spring or summer of 1348. Some sources say that plague got into the country via the port of Bristol, others specify the Melcombe Regis dock area of Weymouth in Dorset; in reality, it probably arrived in various locations on ships carrying goods or returning soldiers from France. From the south, infection spread rapidly north and east, reaching London, East Anglia, the Midlands, Wales and the North. The Scots, maybe keen to capitalise on England's misfortune, raided Durham – which probably assisted the spread of contagion to Scotland, though doubtless it would have got there in its own good time anyway. Infection crossed the water to Ireland. By 1353, it had reached Scandinavia and Russia. It is thought to have begun to subside in Britain, where it is reckoned to have eventually killed about a third of the population – perhaps as many as 2 million people - from about 1350.

This is a truly hideous statistic. Think about it: if that happened today, it would be equivalent to about 19.8 million people dying in Great Britain alone, reducing the population to roughly what it was 100 years ago. Human tragedy aside, how would we cope with that? The emergency services and civil authorities would be overwhelmed – probably similar to the situation in the event of a biological attack. And what would the consequential effects be?

In the worst hit areas of Britain 750 years ago, people

simply did not know what to do. The plague did not discriminate - it could, and did, affect everyone: men, women, young, old, ruling class, clergy and peasants. Society was as dislocated as would be the case today. People must have been terrified. Some, if they could, simply tried to run away from it – possibly the only remedy at the time. Of course, folk did not understand what was happening. They wanted to blame someone, or something, for the dreadful devastation of their communities. Some pointed the finger at Jews (though they had been expelled from England by Edward I a generation earlier) and other minorities, who were often violently persecuted. Some blamed the Church, possibly contributing to a more questioning attitude, the gradual breaking down of social barriers and increasing the potential for unrest, perhaps even revolt. The effects of the pestilence were certainly profound. Some places simply disappeared from the map. Severe labour shortages resulted in higher wages and inflation. But, then, social mobility improved. As less land could be cultivated, sheep farming increased which boosted the wool and cloth trades.

Further outbreaks of plague occurred in Britain in later years, particularly in 1361 and 1374. The last major plague eruption in Britain was the Great Plague of London in 1665 - which also affected other parts of the country.

In Britain, 'The Plague' is a term which usually refers to what people understand to be the bubonic plague, Black Death, or Great Pestilence. It is a disease that primarily affects the black, or ship, rat, *Rattus rattus*, via infected fleas. Having taken in the bacteria *Yersinia Pestis* when biting an infected rat, the flea finds it is unable to ingest and, starving, embarks on a feeding spree, attempting to satiate its hunger. It will feed on any convenient victim – another rat, a human or other mammal, vomiting blood containing the bacteria as it does so, in an attempt to clear its blocked stomach, and passing on Yersinia Pestis in the process. Bubonic plague results from an infection of the lymph nodes, causing painful suppurating bloody-black sores – particularly in the armpits and groin area. Other symptoms include severe pain, fever and gangrene in the extremities (ie toes, fingers, nose). There are two other possible developments. Septicaemic plague is caused when the infection spreads through the body: it ultimately inhibits blood coagulation and is usually fatal because sufferers more or less bleed to death internally. A third form of the plague is pneumonic plague, which is highly aggressive, contagious and almost always fatal. Settling in the lungs, the bacteria cause them to liquefy. Pneumonic plague does not need the assistance of rodents or fleas to spread; it is caught by direct and indirect contact as well as via droplets coughed or sneezed by its dying victims. Some people must be immune, but for most of us anything closer than 12 feet would be deadly.

According to the World Health Organisation, 3,248 cases of the plague were reported worldwide between 2010 and 2015, including 584 deaths.

A violent royal soap opera

Something was wrong with the English monarchy; the only answer seemed to be war

English history in the second half of the 15th century is scarred by civil war - the Wars of the Roses – a label which became popular in Victorian times based on the red and white roses of the rival houses of Lancaster and York. It did not last as long as TV's 'Coronation Street', but it was much more exciting.

The Wars of the Roses was no righteous conflict in a just cause: it was a chain of crude, bloody, dynastic power struggles. First one side, then the other, gained advantage. Adversaries switched allegiances, bumped one another off and did deals behind the scenes. This was the real Game of Thrones, without the dragons and with marginally less gratuitous sex and violence. Just like the fiction, the story is immensely complicated, with a confusing list of *dramatis personae* whose members further obfuscate matters by personal feuds, intermarrying, confusing titles and similar names. What follows is an inadequate summary – but it will give you the general idea.

The chief protagonists in the Wars of the Roses were the descendents of the sons of Edward III, who had died in 1377. Hence, the conflict is also sometimes known as the Cousins' War. The immediate causes of the war stemmed from dissatisfaction with the administration of the country's affairs by the principal councillors of the Lancastrian King, Henry VI, a pious and kindly man who was also inclined to be slightly bonkers. An additional cause of disquiet was the loss of territory in France.

The French set about taking back land won by Henry's warlike father, Henry V. Henry VI favoured peace and, to this end, agreed a 20-year truce (the Treaty of Tours) with the French King Charles VII in 1444. Part of the deal was that Henry would marry Margaret of Anjou – which he duly did the following year – and in return France would receive the provinces of Maine and Anjou. Knowing how immensely unpopular the agreement over Maine and Anjou would be in England, Henry & Co initially kept that particular aspect of the arrangement secret. In fact, the truce did not last anyway. By August 1450, the French had taken Normandy as well - and by 1453 Calais was the only remaining toe-hold England had in France.

A further factor in creating, and maintaining, conflict was the bitter rivalry between different factions of the nobility. The great families of medieval England owned enormous estates, enjoyed immense authority and also had the ability to raise their own private armies – in fact, successive kings relied on them to do just that, in order to fight England's wars. The most powerful families included the Nevilles, earls of Salisbury and Warwick, based in the midlands and the north, and their sworn enemies the Percys, dukes of Northumberland, based in the north east. To illustrate the extreme animosity between these two families, the Percys launched an unprovoked attack on a perfectly innocent Neville wedding party at Heworth Moor (now part of the City of York) in 1453.

Allied to the Nevilles was Richard Plantagenet, Duke of York, an extremely capable commander and administrator. King Henry VI, Richard of York and Henry's favourite advisor, Edmund Beaufort, Duke of Somerset, were all descendants of Edward III and all had, slightly varying, claims to the throne of England. Probably, neither Somerset nor York coveted Henry's throne – he was the anointed king – but there was certainly intense rivalry between the two of them and York felt, with some justification, that Somerset was making a mess of things. The supporters of the 'King's Party' – the Lancastrians – and the 'Things Could Be Better Party' – the Yorkists –

undoubtedly wanted to exploit every opportunity to pursue old vendettas.

Maladministration, high taxes, high prices and the situation in France fed a turbulent undercurrent of unrest and resentment across the land, which encompassed disaffected ex-soldiers, and which sometimes spilled over into lawlessness and agitation. One manifestation of this was the rebellion led by the mysterious Jack Cade in 1450, which culminated in an armed band, said to be thousands strong, mainly from Kent, marching on London. When they got there, they set out demands for reform and hacked off the heads of the Archbishop of Canterbury and the King's treasurer. Some believed Cade's Rebellion was sponsored by York, or his supporters.

In 1453, poor King Henry entered into some kind of catatonic state, a sort of mental oblivion. Parliament appointed York as regent and Somerset was dispatched to the Tower. By all accounts, York ruled wisely in the King's name. But then Henry recovered his senses, freed Somerset and dismissed York. York, his life under threat, summoned his allies Warwick and Salisbury and, in May 1455, marched toward London at the head of 3,000 troops. They met the King heading north with about 2,000 men at St Albans. It is doubtful that York intended to attack the King – he had been sending him messages of loyalty – but some spark resulted in a scuffle, which grew into what history knows as the First Battle of St Albans – and the first battle of the Wars of the Roses. It was a victory for York, largely due to the initiative of Richard Neville, Earl of Warwick, who led his men through the backs of houses to attack the Lancastrians in their flank. Somerset, the Earl of Northumberland and many other Lancastrian nobles were killed. The King was wounded. York assured him of his loyalty and established an uneasy peace which lasted four years.

After that, things got really ugly. The Queen, Margaret

of Anjou, was determined to get rid of York and set about raising an army of 'gallants' personally loyal to her. In 1459, this force intercepted a Yorkist army led by Salisbury at Blore Heath in Staffordshire, which was heading to join York at his castle in Ludlow; again, the Lancastrian forces were trounced. Next, there was a stand-off outside York's Ludlow stronghold: reluctant to fight against the king, some of his troops changed sides; York, Salisbury and Warwick went into exile overseas for awhile. But Margaret engineered Bills of Attainder against York and his supporters – legal devices which effectively declared them guilty of treason and confiscated their estates and revenues, and they had no option but to return to England with an army. The Yorkists won a victory at Northampton in July 1460, where poor, bewildered, Henry was found after the battle in a tent. Margaret headed to Wales, then Scotland, to gather support and inflicted a dramatic defeat on the Yorkists at Wakefield in December, when York himself was killed. His second son, Edmund, and Salisbury were both summarily executed. The heads of all three, with York's wearing a mocking paper crown, were displayed over Micklegate in the City of York.

There seems to be a dreadful inevitability about the Wars of the Roses as the momentum gathers, and the sons of nobles seek to avenge their dead fathers and secure their positions. In February 1461, York's son and heir, the 18-year-old six foot four inch Edward, took terrible revenge on Lancastrian leaders having beaten a Lancastrian army at Mortimer's Cross. Margaret's force, meanwhile, headed for London, looting as it went, and met the Earl of Warwick at St Albans; it was the Lancastrians' turn to win the day and Henry was reunited with his wife. Warwick upped the stakes by declaring York's son, Edward, King Edward IV, in London: so England now had two kings. The rival sides met again at Towton, in Yorkshire, at the end of March, in one of the most terrible battles in English history. It was a resounding defeat for the Lancastrians and, really, it all should have ended there.

Of course, it did not. Margaret wanted to carry on the fight, which she did as best she could in the north. And Edward upset Warwick's carefully arranged plan for a diplomatic marriage to a French princess by announcing he was already married to Elizabeth Woodville, a beautiful commoner. When York filled court with Elizabeth's relatives (who had previously backed the Lancastrians), the humiliated Warwick joined his erstwhile bitter enemy, Margaret. In 1470, Edward was forced to flee the country and Henry was once again restored to the throne. Richard Neville, Earl of Warwick, is known to history as 'the Kingmaker'.

But, dear reader, inevitably York returned. Gathering a new army, he defeated Warwick's troops at Barnet in April 1471 and his old friend and mentor was killed in the fighting. Margaret then headed west, to assemble more troops. Swiftly, Edward followed and at Tewkesbury on 4 May inflicted a further bloody defeat on the Lancastrians. The slaughter continued into the nave of Tewkesbury Abbey and included Margaret and King Henry's 17-year old son and heir, Edward of Westminster, the Prince of Wales. Edward IV returned to London, where poor old King Henry was quietly murdered in the Tower, probably with a blow to the back of the head.

For a while, apart from Edward feeling the need to bump off his treacherous brother the Duke of Clarence (who is meant to have been drowned in a butt of Malmsey wine), that was that. Edward has a reputation as a fair monarch (relatively speaking) and England prospered. Then, in 1483, he died, possibly of a stroke, possibly typhoid, aged just 40. Enter centre stage Edward's younger brother, Richard, Duke of Gloucester…

Of course, Richard had been by Edward's side for sometime. He had married one of Warwick's daughters,

Anne Neville, acquiring a huge fortune in the process, and more or less ruled the north of England. Richard seized Edward and Elizabeth's sons, his nephews, 12-year old Edward – the uncrowned King Edward V – and his 9-year old brother, Richard. The young princes were taken to the Tower of London 'for safety' - and never seen again. Parliament, at the bidding of Richard's allies, had the boys declared illegitimate on the grounds that their father was already married before he married Elizabeth Woodville, and 'called on' Gloucester to become king. He was duly crowned King Richard III.

The stage was set for the final chapter in this awful, but fascinating, saga. Forces were gathering against Richard, clustering around a 28-year old Lancastrian, Henry Tudor – another descendant of Edward III – who had been biding his time in exile in Brittany. Henry landed at Milford Haven in August 1485 with a small force and, gathering support along the way, met the King's army at Bosworth in the English Midlands on 22 August. Richard, deserted by his ally Lord Stanley (who happened to be married to Henry Tudor's mother, Margaret Beaufort), fought bravely, but was cut down. According to legend, his crown was retrieved from a thorn bush by Stanley and placed on Henry's head. Richard's corpse was stripped, paraded through nearby Leicester and found under a car park 500 or so years later.

Henry Tudor began a new dynasty as Henry VII. He married Elizabeth of York, daughter of Edward IV and Elizabeth Woodville, thereby uniting Lancaster and York. The conjoined red and white roses – the Tudor rose – can be seen all over the country even today. Their son, Henry VIII, changed England – and Britain – for ever. Nowadays, the rivalry between Lancaster and York is limited to county cricket; and in Tudor Britain we can see the foundations for much of our modern world.

4 THE TUDORS

The victor of Bosworth

New dynasty, fresh start?

There was by no means unanimous agreement that the new Tudor King, Henry VII, had the best claim to the throne of England in 1485. In fact, depending on your point of view, his claim could be considered quite flimsy. Henry was the son of a formidable mother, Margaret Beaufort, and Edmund Tudor. Margaret was the great-great-granddaughter of John of Gaunt, Edward III's third surviving son, and his mistress, Katherine Swynford. John and Katherine later married, but their children were often declared illegitimate – legitimacy was pretty important when it came to royal lineage. Henry's father, Edmund Tudor, was the son of Catherine of Valois (Henry V's royal French wife) and Owen Tudor, a Welsh courtier. So Henry VII was Edward III's great-great-great-grandson through his mother.

But, given that many of those with a claim to the English throne were dead, or missing, and that Henry had just beaten the sitting king, Richard, at the Battle of Bosworth, there were limited options.

Among the more bizarre attempted rebellions in British history were the cases of Lambert Simnel and Perkin Warbeck (or was it Lambert Warbeck and Perkin Simnel?). Ten year-old Lambert Simnel was first considered by his supporters as being Richard of York, the younger of the two princes in the Tower; then, it was suggested he was the Earl of Warwick, nephew to Edward IV. In any event, he was crowned king in Dublin, his rebel army duly landed in 1487 in the north of England, at Furness, and proceeded to make its way southward in the general direction of London.

It was halted and thoroughly beaten by Henry's forces near Newark. Simnel, who Henry recognised as being a mere pawn in the whole affair, was put to work in the royal kitchens, where I gather he did quite well. Perkin Warbeck was a slightly different proposition. Claiming to be Richard of York (again), he made various attempts to invade with the support of gullible, or perhaps hopeful, allies in France, Ireland and Scotland, and even managed to marry a Scottish princess. However, he was captured following one of these attempts and executed in 1499.

If Henry had a mission, though, it was 'recovery' after the many years of war – peace and reconciliation, if you like. His marriage to Elizabeth of York, daughter of Edward IV and Elizabeth Woodville, was a good move in uniting the houses of Lancaster and York. The Tudor rose, combining the red rose of Lancaster with the white rose of York, was a neat piece of propaganda, and branding. Henry enjoyed administration – his hand is all over documents in the National Archives. Though he has a reputation for being obsessed with money, he left England a more secure, stable, place than it had been for a very long time indeed, as well as with a full royal treasury. He seems to have been cautious abroad – though he did sponsor the Genoese explorer, John Cabot, to investigate the New World, which resulted in the Tudor flag being planted in Nova Scotia.

One of Henry's daughters, Margaret, married King James VI of Scotland (remember that – she was Mary Queen of Scots' grandmother) and another daughter, Mary, married the elderly Louis XII of France (though he died, perhaps exhausted, after three months). Henry's son and heir, Arthur (named after the legendary British hero), married one of the catches of Europe, Katherine of Aragon. However, Arthur's premature death at the age of 15 necessitated a re-think on the part of the king and his advisers. Rather than return the young widow, and her dowry, to Spain, Katherine was betrothed to Arthur's younger brother, ten-year old Henry. And it was young Henry Tudor who took the throne as Henry VIII in 1509, when his father died. He was just short of 18 years old and had an interesting future ahead of him.

Losing our religion

How Henry VIII changed the world and his wife

No challenge blighted Henry VIII's accession to the English throne. The country was at peace and it seemed to be a golden age. In contrast to the ailing, bloated, tyrant he was to become, the youthful king is often portrayed as a true renaissance prince – a modern man of his time. He was handsome (apparently), athletic, well-educated, a patron of the arts and a lover of warfare, rapidly spending the treasure so carefully gathered by his father. He fought and beat both the French and Scots - his sister Margaret's husband, James IV of Scotland was killed at the Battle of Flodden Field, near Branxton in Northumberland, in 1513 - and he boxed above his weight by attempting to influence the balance of power in Europe between France and the Holy Roman Empire (Austria, Spain, the Netherlands and Italy).

People may remember King Henry VIII as the one with the six wives: Katherine of Aragon – divorced; Anne Boleyn – beheaded; Jane Seymour – died; Anne of Cleves – divorced; Catherine Howard – beheaded; Catherine Parr – survived. But his lasting legacy was the break with the Church – the Catholic Church - which had wielded enormous political and social power, not always benignly, throughout medieval Europe.

These events define Henry VIII's reign for many people. But it took Henry 18 years to realise that he didn't want to stay married to the first Mrs Tudor, Katherine of Aragon, his brother's widow. Katherine had produced a daughter, Mary – who by all accounts Henry adored. And Henry had an illegitimate son, the subtly named Henry Fitzroy (Fitzroy means 'son of the king'), with his mistress Elizabeth Blount. But his marriage with Katherine had failed to provide a surviving legitimate male heir – and that's what Henry really wanted. Perhaps, he thought, there was something wrong with Katherine (it couldn't possibly be him); or perhaps they could not have a son because it had been a sin to marry his brother's wife. Henry's obsession with being able to pass the crown on to a son might be explained not just as mere ego, but also as a desire to avoid the chaos and anarchy of previous reigns, so often brought about by a crisis in succession. Which sounds fair enough.

However, Henry also had a roving eye and several mistresses. Katherine, aging and probably worn out by living in Tudor Britain as well as several miscarriages, was perhaps less alluring than one of her ladies in waiting, the saucy-eyed Anne Boleyn, sister of another of Henry's conquests, Mary. Anne, however, played hard to get; she would not share his bed while he was still married to Katherine. The fate of a nation turned on a man's lust and a woman's sexual scruple – or can we say naked ambition?

Up to that point, Henry had been as keen a Roman Catholic as he was expected to be. In 1521, having written a pamphlet against the views of the German reformer, Martin Luther, the Pope even appointed Henry 'Defender of the Faith' – a title still used by monarchs of the UK. But the Pope would not give Henry a divorce, partly for fear of upsetting Charles V, the Holy Roman Emperor - who happened to be Katherine of Aragon's nephew - even though there were possible theological grounds for annulment because she had been his brother's widow. If Henry became head of a church of England, though, anything was possible; who needed a Pope, then? - goodness, his own Archbishop of Canterbury could grant him a divorce!

Thus was conceived the English Reformation, eventually making England a Protestant country and precipitating all manner of unpleasantness in the process. Be clear; the course of history was re-written, not because of any particular religious zeal or alleged moral imperative, but as a matter of expediency, to enable Henry to get his own way. Henry simply jumped on the convenient bandwagon of a wider movement for religious reform. The Act of Supremacy in 1534 created the Church of England and made Henry its head – and as a consequence Britain changed forever. It also meant that anyone who refused to swear an oath accepting Henry's position – like a religious dissenter, for example, or his erstwhile friend and minister, Thomas More – could be guilty of treason and executed. Consequently, the last decade of Henry's reign was undoubtedly a period of terror.

Henry's principal advisors were now more likely to be laymen – men like More, and his successor, Thomas Cromwell – than men of the cloth, like his previous Lord Chancellor, Cardinal Thomas Wolsey, who was discredited for failing to get the divorce that Henry wanted. The break with Rome also proved to be a catalyst for dissolving some 800 Catholic monasteries, a policy which offered a neat, and opportunist, prospect for wealth creation as well as ridding the land of allegedly corrupt institutions. Further, selling off monastic lands to merchants and others brought new landowners onto the king's side, whilst simultaneously providing a fillip for the burgeoning middle-class. Most of the monks and nuns were treated relatively well and given pensions, though any who objected could expect extremely harsh treatment, including a gruesome execution – and there were several of those. However, one consequence of the dissolution – apart from the cultural vandalism that Henry is often accused of – is the gap that the removal of monasteries left in communities and society in general. Whatever failings monasteries had (and there were a few), it has been claimed that their passing set English society back many years, because the monasteries had provided rudimentary education, health care and social welfare and there was no plan to fill the vacuum left by their departure. Some might argue that society is still having this debate.

Unfortunately, and ironically, Anne did not bear Henry a son either; though she did give birth to a rather memorable daughter, Elizabeth. Henry did finally get his legitimate son and heir, the traditionally alleged sickly Edward born to his third wife, Jane Seymour, who died shortly after giving birth. Edward succeeded his father, aged just nine years, in 1547.

In 1536, the Laws in Wales Act was introduced. Often incorrectly referred to as the 'Act of Union' between England and Wales, it abolished the powerful Marcher Lords put in place by William the Conqueror, established Welsh administrative areas and MPs and aimed to harmonise Welsh administration and law with English. Whilst possibly well-intentioned, this legislation did not receive universal approval – not least because it determined that English would be the only language of the courts of Wales, and Welsh speakers – which meant most of the population of Wales - could not hold public office.

In 1541, Henry VIII appointed himself King of Ireland. Irish lords were persuaded to give up their Gaelic titles and lands and instead hold them, with new English titles, as effective vassals of the King of England. Understandably, the Irish rebelled against English (and Protestant) rule – and Irish wars thenceforward became a feature of the Tudor period and beyond.

Henry tried to persuade his nephew, James V of Scotland, to follow his lead and break with Rome. James's refusal provoked an irritated Henry to send a wrecking army into the borders. In return, James invaded England with a large force, which was roundly defeated at the Battle of Solway Moss in 1542. The following year, representatives of both countries concluded the Treaty of Greenwich, which not only made peace, but also agreed to a union of the crowns by the marriage of the infant Queen Mary of Scotland to Henry's son, Edward. The Scottish

Parliament later repudiated the agreement and Henry set about achieving his objectives by force, invading again in 1544. This extremely violent, unsuccessful, attempt to force an alliance with Scotland is colourfully known as 'the rough wooing.'

Yet Henry left England relatively strong, and he had cultivated an interest in the navy - which did no harm for an island nation potentially isolated, cut adrift from its traditional Catholic roots, that may have need to rely on its maritime skills. In fact, he may have created and made himself head of the Church of England, but, when Henry died in 1547, at heart he was still the Catholic he had always been. It was his son Edward VI's brief reign that seriously advanced the cause of Protestantism in Britain, as wild-eyed evangelicals removed images from churches, smashed stained glass, destroyed relics and whitewashed over walls. In 1549, Archbishop Thomas Cranmer, one of the architects of the English Reformation, published the Book of Common Prayer and its use was imposed throughout the country. Then, in the summer of 1553, the fifteen-year old king died – probably from tuberculosis.

Edward's rightful successor was his thirty-seven year old half-sister, Mary – the fruit of his father's first marriage. But she was a Catholic and Edward had named the freckle-faced teenager Lady Jane Grey, an impeccable Protestant and cousin of the Duke of Northumberland, Edward's chief minister, to succeed him. She was queen for just nine days. While Northumberland took a force to East Anglia to capture Mary, nobles and Privy Councillors vacillated, changed their minds, imprisoned Jane in the Tower and declared Mary queen. Northumberland was executed – as was, later, poor sixteen-year old Lady Jane Grey.

Mary set about a Counter-Reformation, restoring Catholic rituals and imprisoning leading Protestants on charges of heresy. She even married Philip of Spain, heir to Europe's most powerful Catholic state, causing some resentment and making many of her countrymen fearful of foreign takeover. Mary sought to purge her land of Protestantism, burning bishops Latimer and Ridley, followed by Archbishop Cranmer, at the stake in Oxford; you can still see the spot where this happened.

Religious persecution took many forms in the Tudor period; at its most extreme, people were tortured horrifically in an effort to persuade them to recant (or deny) their beliefs. If that didn't work, they could be burned alive. Burnings always took place in public and invariably on market days to attract maximum exposure, thereby in theory acting as a deterrent. Of the almost 400 people estimated to have been burned as heretics in England and Wales throughout the Tudor period, the vast majority were Protestants and most of those were burned during Mary's 5-year reign. But Mary could never completely reverse the Reformation; the horse had already bolted and most people had little appetite for restoring the authority of Rome, which was viewed as foreign and therefore unacceptable. In the last year of her tenure on England's throne, the French took Calais, the final remnant of a once significant European empire and, until 1558, as English as Portsmouth. Mary went to her grave in November that year, knowing that her half-sister, Elizabeth, would succeed her and that her Catholic Counter-Reformation had failed.

Dawn of Empire

The roots of modern Britain

Somehow, Elizabethan England has a very different atmosphere to any previous period in British history. Queen Elizabeth I succeeded to the throne on the death of her elder Catholic half-sister 'Bloody' Mary in 1558. She was twenty-five. Her 45 year rule is popularly seen as heralding a new age for England and she has been described as one of the country's greatest monarchs. The Elizabethan age witnessed the exploration of the New World, war with maritime rivals such as Spain (including an attempted invasion), Europe's introduction to hitherto unknown species and consumables, such as turkeys, tobacco and potatoes – and the beginnings of the British Empire. The British East India Company received its charter from Elizabeth in 1600; its influence on future British control in India was profound. Shakespeare, arguably England's greatest playwright, was in his ascendancy during the latter part of Elizabeth's reign. And the Queen's refusal to marry and the consequent lack of a Tudor heir, whether by fate or design, paved the way for the unification of the crowns of England and Scotland.

Elizabeth was Henry VIII's second daughter; her mother was Anne Boleyn. After the death of her young half-brother, Edward VI, Elizabeth became a potential magnet for Protestant supporters and did well to survive during Mary's brutal attempt to restore England to Catholicism. She inherited a country torn by religious faction. Whilst re-establishing the Church of England, Elizabeth set out to follow what could be described as a moderate Protestant line. Initially, she tried to steer clear of religious wars that were tearing neighbouring countries apart. Though suspicions of Catholic intentions remained, and these undoubtedly influenced decision-making, the extremes of general religious intolerance that had been a hallmark of the three previous reigns should have gradually disappeared.

The Acts of Supremacy and Uniformity in 1559 confirmed Elizabeth as Supreme Head of the Church of England and re-established a Protestant Common Prayer Book. Fines could be imposed on those who failed to attend services at their parish church. As during the time of Henry VIII, holders of public office were required to swear an oath of loyalty to the Sovereign as head of the Church. Clearly, none of this was acceptable to a true Catholic, but Elizabeth was not overly bothered about people's private beliefs, provided they were loyal to her; and most Catholics did enough to steer clear of trouble. However, many Catholics regarded Elizabeth as a bastard who should not be sitting on England's throne at all, and the Queen spent much of her reign in danger.

The focus of Catholic plots against Elizabeth, and there were several, was her Catholic cousin, Mary, Queen of Scots. Mary was one of the stars of the age. Queen of Scotland at six days old, she was raised at the French court, married to the dauphin (heir to the French throne) at fifteen and, when his father died the following year, in 1559, she became Queen of France too. She was also Henry VII's great-granddaughter and, as such, had a strong claim to the throne of England. Things could have turned out so very differently. The early death of her husband precipitated a return to her homeland in 1561, which she found divided over religion. The Reformation did not arrive in Scotland at the behest of the monarch, as it had in England, but through the actions of zealous reformers like George Wishart and his disciple, the radical Calvinist John Knox. Protestant pressure and a chaotic personal life would be the young Scottish Queen's undoing. Mary's Catholic second husband, Henry Stuart, Lord Darnley, was unpopular, unbalanced and arrogant. Aggrieved at Mary's refusal to appoint him co-ruler, and jealous of her friendship with her secretary, David Rizzio, he joined a group of Protestant protestors who brutally murdered Rizzio in front of a pregnant Mary in Holyrood Palace. Three months later, the Queen gave birth to her son, James. The following year, 1567, Darnley was himself murdered – blown up and smothered (or maybe the other way round). Suspicion fell on Mary and a new favourite, James Hepburn, the Earl of Bothwell. Three months after Darnley's assassination, Mary married Bothwell. It was all too much for the Scottish nobility, who deposed Mary in favour of her infant son. Imprisonment in Loch Leven Castle followed and, following her dramatic escape from captivity in 1568 and the subsequent defeat of her forces at the Battle of Langside in Glasgow, Mary sought refuge in England. However, Elizabeth had her cousin held captive, albeit in relative comfort and allowing her the dignity of a queen, in a succession of fortresses for the next nineteen years. During that time, the idea of Mary grabbing the throne of England became an objective for ever disgruntled Catholic plotters.

Catholicism was more entrenched in the north of England and a rebellion there in 1569, the so-called 'Revolt of the Northern Earls', was one unsuccessful attempt to replace Elizabeth with Mary. The tension ratcheted up even more in 1570 when the Pope issued a bull – a decree - *Regnans in Exclesis*, which excommunicated Elizabeth, declared her a heretic and released her Catholic subjects from any allegiance to her. This effectively pronounced open season on the Queen of England and was catastrophic for English Catholics, since it turned all of them into potential traitors. The issue was particularly sensitive as England's No 1 Enemy by this time was Catholic Spain, ruled by King Philip II – who you may remember had married Elizabeth's predecessor and half-sister Mary, and who therefore might have once considered himself King of

England. In 1586, Elizabeth's spymaster, Francis Walsingham, uncovered another plot, the Babington Plot, to exchange an assassinated Elizabeth for the Scottish queen, which unquestionably implicated Mary. Elizabeth was eventually persuaded to sign the warrant for her cousin's execution, which was dramatically carried out – allegedly without Elizabeth's reluctant final permission - at Fotheringhay Castle on 8 February 1587.

Attitudes toward Catholics understandably hardened after 1570, particularly with the arrival in England of specially trained, highly educated, Jesuit missionary priests who were dedicated to replacing the Church of England with Roman Catholicism. Such priests were deemed guilty of treason. The penalties for hearing Mass or not attending church were increased. The priests, and anyone sheltering them, could suffer extreme penalties. Although, fortunately, Elizabeth refused to be panicked into believing that all English Catholics were traitors, many priests and laymen were grimly executed.

Christopher Columbus' trip to what he misnamed the West Indies in 1492 had encouraged great interest in the Americas by the primary maritime powers – Spain, Portugal, France – and England. The potential for wealth and power was clear and 'Good Queen Bess' encouraged explorers and adventurers such as Richard Grenville, John Hawkins, Walter Raleigh and Francis Drake. Beyond these shores, they were often regarded as pirates; maybe so – but they were our pirates! It was all very heroic, were it not for the eternal blemish on the reputations of many of the remarkable men involved, including Sir Francis Drake, for their involvement in founding the slave trade in America. West Africans were abducted, usually with the connivance of local chiefs, and shipped to the New World where they were sold to settlers of all nations.

Amongst Drake's more worthy achievements was the

part he played in the defeat of the Spanish Armada. To put this in context, the purpose of the Armada, sponsored by our friend King Philip, was to invade, topple the heretic queen Elizabeth and conquer England. The invasion had been expected. In 1587, Drake sailed into Cadiz harbour and destroyed a good part of Spain's navy, declaring that he had "singed the King of Spain's beard". But this merely delayed the inevitable and, by July 1588, Philip had replenished his fleet. Some 150 ships and 26,000 men set sail for England via the Netherlands, where they were to be joined by 30,000 more soldiers. However, that rendezvous never took place. Harried by the smaller and more manoeuvrable English ships, outclassed in terms of leadership, hampered by poor communications and finally the victims of appalling weather and heavy seas, which claimed most of the Spanish fleet, the attempted invasion failed and an estimated 20,000 Spaniards lost their lives. It was one of the greatest English victories in history and a primary reason why bull fighting never caught on in Neasden. At Tilbury, Elizabeth told troops assembled to repel the invasion, "I know I have the body but of a weak and feeble woman; but I have the heart and stomach of a king, and of a king of England too".

Much has been written about Elizabeth's refusal to marry, despite being under considerable pressure from her advisors to do so in order to secure the succession with an heir. She is said to have been a passionate woman, loved the attention of young men and had several favourites – not least Robert Dudley, who she created 1st Earl of Leicester and whose last letter she kept until her death. Perhaps Elizabeth knew better than anyone, though: a husband, whether English or foreign, would risk upsetting one faction or another, or becoming embroiled in overseas entanglements that England could ill-afford at the time.

In any event, Elizabeth died childless, after catching a

chill, at Richmond Palace in 1603. It was the end of the Tudors. Elizabeth was also the last English monarch of the English nation. At 36, her cousin, King James VI of Scotland, the son that Catholic Mary Queen of Scots had left behind, additionally became King James I of England. James had been raised a Protestant. He had supported Elizabeth against France and Spain. He was the great-great grandson of Henry VII; though the states remained separate, the thrones of England and Scotland were finally joined.

5 THE STUARTS

The Stuarts and the Republic

Two immovable objects collide - the monarch and parliament

James Stuart, the new King James I of England in 1603, had been King James VI of Scotland since 1567. And he had a pretty good pedigree: as well as being the great-grandson of James IV and Margaret Tudor, he was the direct descendent of Robert the Bruce. A Stuart had sat on the Scottish throne since 1371 and you can't help wondering what went through James's mind as he approached the centre of power of his country's auld enemy, knowing that their top job was now his.

Historians often do not regard James I (or VI) too favourably. He has been called 'The wisest fool in Christendom', a man who never said a foolish thing nor ever did a wise one. He has also been described as 'slobbering' and 'spluttering' and, generally, seems to have been somewhat unpleasant in his personal habits. He certainly had a knack for upsetting people at the time. The English resented the influx of Scots at Court; the Scots left behind felt abandoned (James only returned to Scotland once after becoming king of England); and everyone came to resent the influence of his favourites, the most notable of which was George Villiers, who James created Earl and, ultimately, Duke, of Buckingham. Of course, James came from a broken home: his father, Lord Darnley, was a pompous ass, a murderer and was himself murdered not long after James was born; his mother, Mary, Queen of Scots, who he can't have had any memory of, was executed on the orders of James's English predecessor, Elizabeth. As if that wasn't enough emotional baggage for any child, he had suffered through four regents ruling Scotland on his behalf until he came of age, as well as imprisonment, assault and a sadistic tutor. If anyone needed friends, it was James.

But James was also intelligent, well-read and ambitious. He had a vision, too: more than just a unified crown, he wanted to create a unified nation, Great Britain. He even came up with a banner, a forerunner of today's Union flag. Possibly fearing loss of identity and independence, the idea of a union of nations was rejected by English and Scots alike.

James had developed some strong views, which included an intense dislike of tobacco and smoking, and a deep-seated concern about the dangers of witchcraft. He was also a believer in the principle of the Divine Right of Kings – a doctrine that he passed on to his unfortunate son, Charles. Thinking you have the ear of a deity is usually a dangerous assumption, often ending in tears; believing that you receive your power through God too might make a chap a little conceited, and even a tad inflexible. You might also argue that the Scottish Stuarts had no direct experience of the principles behind Magna Carta.

On the positive side, one of his first acts as James I was to conclude peace with Spain. He also ordered a new translation of the Bible into English. The work of 50-plus scholars and published in 1611, The King James Bible is still regarded as a masterpiece 500 years later and its turn of phrase enriches our language every day.

Though raised a Protestant, James could be sympathetic to Catholics; his wife, Anne of Denmark, was one. But Catholics were still persecuted, and widely regarded with suspicion by the Protestant majority. Disappointed not to receive the tolerance they had expected under the new king, a bunch of English Catholic extremists, led by a charismatic nobleman called Robert Catesby, hatched a revolutionary plot. Their idea was to blow up Parliament with James and everyone else in it on 5 November 1605, and replace the King with his daughter, the Princess Elizabeth (who knew nothing about it). One Guido Fawkes was chosen to lay the gunpowder. They were betrayed (inevitably), some were killed in a fire-fight (heroically), the survivors tortured horribly (of course), and then executed in the most unpleasant manner imaginable by being hanged, drawn and quartered. Bonfires have been lit throughout the land on 5 November ever since to mark the event. But be in no doubt, the Gunpowder Plot was a planned act of terrorism on a par with many launched by nationalist and religious extremists in modern times; had it succeeded, the casualties would have been horrendous and the consequences profound. As it was, it set the cause of moderate British Catholics back years.

James was even-handed, though; radical Protestants – 'Puritans' – were persecuted too. A group of fundamentalist Protestants felt sufficiently victimised to start a new life in the New World, setting sail on the Mayflower on 16 September 1620 and landing at Cape Cod on 21 November. They became known as the Pilgrim Fathers. In fact, the first permanent British colony in North America had been founded in 1607 at Jamestown – named after the King. By the end of James's reign, some 80,000 Britons had crossed the Atlantic to start new lives in America: not all were religious refugees; some were escaping economic hardship.

Some bright spark also hit on a cunning scheme to encourage Scottish Protestants to settle land in Ireland that had been confiscated from Catholics. The so-called 'Plantation of Ulster' in 1609 was possibly not one of His Majesty's Government's better ideas and, of course, the consequences of it remain with us to this day.

Given his beliefs, James did not have much time for Parliament; he seems to have viewed its purpose as being primarily to approve his extravagant spending. However, his son Charles, who succeeded his father in 1625, had a spectacular falling-out with it. Charles was a cultured man, and an avid art collector, but not particularly bright. One of his first mistakes, in the circumstances, was to marry a very forthright French Catholic, Henrietta Maria. His continued reliance on his father's favourite, the Duke of Buckingham, was deeply unpopular – though Buckingham's influence ended abruptly when he was murdered by a disaffected army officer in Portsmouth in 1628. Charles's poor relationship with a strongly Protestant, and increasingly independent, Parliament resulted in the 1628 Petition of Right, which told the King that he could not tax without the will of the Commons, or imprison without trial. Charles, of course, considered himself accountable to no one but God. So he dismissed Parliament and tried to rule without it, raising money by any means he could. This included reviving an old levy called 'ship tax'. Originally paid by coastal towns and intended to help fund their defence, the King applied it nationwide – to widespread howls of protest.

The King also sought to impose a new 'high church' (ie quasi-Catholic) prayer-book on Presbyterian Scotland. It was too much, resulting in riots in Edinburgh and the declaration of the National Covenant in 1638, opposing the King's interference. The 'Covenanters', as they became known, simply would not accept any King attempting to be head of their church. Charles declared what became known as 'the Bishops' War' on Scotland, which went badly for him and ended up with the Scots occupying Newcastle upon Tyne. The conflict also marked the opening shots in what would become a much wider civil war. Desperate for money, the King summoned the English Parliament. Parliament revised its earlier Petition of Right into a 200-clause 'Grand Remonstrance', which was so radical that, even now, it has not been fully acted upon. In January 1642, Charles entered Parliament and vainly attempted to arrest those that he saw as the ringleaders. Armed bands sympathetic to Parliament sought the Queen, who was perceived to be a bad influence. It seems that Charles and Henrietta were genuinely fond of one another. They parted, she heading for the safety of France and the King to Nottingham where, on 22 August, he raised his standard and summoned his subjects to defend their king. Civil War had returned to Britain.

The war that is generally known as the English Civil War was more accurately British, because although much of the initial fighting took place in England, the whole of Britain was involved. It was a tragic war, as if there is any other kind, setting friends, sons, fathers and brothers against each other. Estimates of those killed range from 200,000 to 300,000 people, including non-combatants. Yet the war was one of the prime shapers of modern Britain, an intense power struggle that ultimately determined how its nations would be governed. The final outcome was a revolution; never again could the monarchy directly challenge the will of Parliament - well, not without provoking a crisis, anyway. It was a significant step toward a parliamentary democracy with a constitutional monarch.

Factional support during the Civil War was more or less regional, with the Parliamentarians, or 'Roundheads' (because some of them sported shorter hair) stronger in the wealthier and typically more radical south-east and London. The rest of England generally sided with the King. There were religious divisions too: puritanical Protestants supported Parliament; Catholics fought for the Royalists. It wasn't that simple, of course; but it will do for our purposes.

Initially, the Royalists, or 'Cavaliers' (originally a term of ridicule, derived from the French *chevalier*, for knight) did quite well. But the King's forces were in due course defeated by better organised, better supplied and better disciplined Parliament armies under Thomas Fairfax and

Oliver Cromwell (one time MP for Huntingdon, like ex-Prime Minister John Major). From 1643, the Parliamentary cause benefitted significantly from Scottish troops, fighting in return for the undertaking that Scottish Presbyterianism would be adopted in England – a promise that wasn't kept. In response to what was perceived as poor military performance, Parliament also formed what history has called, 'the New Model Army', Britain's first trained professional fighting force. This was theoretically apolitical, with officers selected on merit, rather than title. Every infantryman wore a scarlet tunic, red being the cheapest dye. Thus was born the British 'redcoat', the standard uniform colour of the British Army until khaki was introduced in the 19th century.

The Battle of Naseby in 1645 was a decisive victory for the Parliamentary cause. Later the Scots, beguiled by Charles's promises, changed sides and were in turn defeated by Cromwell at Preston in 1648. Charles was handed over to Parliament by the Scots, and brought to trial by a specially convened commission who found him guilty of treason and required that "his head be severed from his body." Charles, wearing an extra shirt ("were I to shake through cold, my enemies would attribute it to fear"), was beheaded at Whitehall on a cold January day in 1649. The King, believing in the Divine Right of Kings, never accepted the validity of the process that took his life with just one blow. As the executioner held up the head and announced, "Behold, the head of a traitor!" one eyewitness remarked that "there was such a groan by the thousands then present, as I never heard before and desire I may never hear again." Killing an anointed monarch was a step too far for many.

Still, the office of king was abolished and England, along with Wales, was declared a republic. No one had consulted Scotland about the execution of their king. Five days afterwards, the Scots declared his son Charles II, King of

Scotland, Ireland and England. Parliament dispatched Oliver Cromwell to Ireland and Scotland, to snuff out further Royalist unrest, which he did with considerable severity. He is despised in Ireland, even today. The Scots crowned Charles's son Charles II in 1651; this further attempted counter-revolution was decisively beaten – again by Cromwell - at Worcester. Charles fled into exile, having famously hidden in an oak tree at Boscobel House near Wolverhampton along the way.

There was no model for future government, but there were deep religious and political differences amongst Members of Parliament and the army. Cromwell dominated affairs, grew impatient, disbanded Parliament, tried to persuade 140 "God-fearing men" representing "the various forms of Godliness in this nation" to devise a constitution and, when that failed, was persuaded to take on the mantle of monarch – but not king – in the form of 'Lord Protector of the Commonwealth'. His over-arching objective in this period seems to have been to achieve stability after the war, "healing and settling", as he called it, which included religious tolerance for all but those Cromwell considered most extreme. Like Charles I, Cromwell might have seen himself as being on a divine mission. He encouraged Jews, who had been banished from England almost 400 years earlier by Edward I, to return. Contrary to pub quizzes, he did not personally ban Christmas; Parliament had been clamping down on what were seen as Catholic excesses and rituals in the celebration of Christmas and other holy days since the 1640s. Ultimately, an ordinance of 1645 confirmed the abolition of the feasts of Christmas, Easter and Whitsun; so, until the Restoration in 1660, celebrating Christmas was officially illegal and Cromwell probably supported that. Abroad, Cromwell made peace with the Dutch, allied the Commonwealth with France against Spain, and captured Jamaica. However, Cromwell's rule was largely possible only with the support of the army – which has given the British a deep-seated suspicion of militarism.

No one really knew what to do after Cromwell's death in 1658. His son, Richard, briefly succeeded him; but did not carry sufficient personal authority. The prospect of anarchy loomed. Up stepped General George Monck, Cromwell's Governor in Scotland. Monck marched south at the head of an army, crossing the border at Coldstream – thus accidentally forming the Coldstream Guards in the process. In London, he recognised that the only way forward was a form of popular monarchy – and the best candidate seemed to be the exiled Charles II.

Restoration and Glorious Revolution

Hedonism, big hair and the end of Popery

Negotiations with the exiled Charles II in March 1660 resulted in the Declaration of Breda, in which the king promised a general pardon for those that had participated in the civil war, a degree of religious toleration, acceptance of the supremacy of Parliament and the settlement of soldiers' pay. On 8 May 1660, Charles II was formally proclaimed King in London. He landed at Dover on 25 May and arrived in London on 29 May, his 30th birthday.

Charles' general pardon excluded those deemed guilty of regicide – killing his father, Charles I. Those still living were hunted down: some were gruesomely executed, some imprisoned, others fled into exile. The body of Oliver Cromwell, and the corpses of other dead prominent parliamentarians, were exhumed, posthumously hanged and decapitated, their heads exhibited on poles and their bodies thrown into an anonymous pit.

But for most people, the Restoration was an opportunity for reconciliation and was greeted with enthusiastic delight. The personality of the 'merrie monarch', debonair, extrovert, extravagant and highly promiscuous, is stamped all over his reign, contrasting with the apparent greyness and uncertainty of the previous two decades. Charles II supported the new Royal Society, whose illustrious members included Isaac Newton, Christopher Wren and Robert Boyle. But it wasn't all positive. There was war with the Dutch, who burned 13 ships in Chatham harbour and towed away the Navy's flagship, Royal Charles. This provided a catalyst for major naval reforms, responsibly managed by one Samuel Pepys - probably better known now for his diary. The Great Plague of 1665 was devastating – an estimated 100,000 people died in London, though the horror was by no means restricted to the capital.

This was followed in London by the Great Fire the following year, which largely destroyed the medieval city and changed the capital for ever.

Differences in religion – or at any rate suspicion of Catholicism - still cast a shadow over affairs. Charles was inclined to be tolerant of Catholics – and actually converted on his death-bed. However, in 1673, Parliament passed the Test Act, banning Catholics from public office. Anti-Catholic hysteria, never far beneath the surface, was whipped to a frenzy by the false claims of an unsavoury con-artist with the natty name of Titus Oates. His fictional 'Popish Plot' of 1678 warned of arson attacks on London and a conspiracy to replace Charles with his Roman Catholic brother, James, the Duke of York. Oates' false accusations resulted in the arrest and deaths of many innocent Catholics – he was later imprisoned by James II, but released and given a pension by WilliamandMary (aka William and Mary).

It was around this time that political factions began to emerge – forerunners of modern political parties. On the one hand were the 'Tories' – broadly royalist in sympathies – and on the other were the 'Whigs' – generally protestant or anti-Catholic parliamentarians. Both were originally mutually abusive terms and extensions of the lines drawn in the Civil War. 'Tory' is said to derive from an Irish term for a bunch of Catholic outlaws, *toruigh*; 'Whig' possibly comes from a Scottish term, *whiggam-more*, meaning 'pack-saddle thieves'.

Charles is well known for his innumerable mistresses, including the infamous Nell Gwynne. Though they possibly didn't contribute much to Britain, these ladies helped keep a smile on the King's face. The King's last words are reputed to have been, "Let not poor Nelly starve."

Because Charles had no legitimate heirs (though he had

plenty of illegitimate ones), when the King died in February 1685 his brother, the openly Catholic James, succeeded him to the throne as James II of England and VII of Scotland. James had had a successful public life as the Duke of York since the Restoration, busying himself with naval and colonial matters – and winning admiration for helping to personally lead the fight against the Great Fire of London in 1666. In 1664, New York was named after him – not after the city in Yorkshire, as is often believed.

However, James's succession to the throne was regarded with considerable suspicion by some Protestants, who regarded him, with justification, as naturally pro-Catholic and possibly pro-French. In June 1685, the Duke of Monmouth, the oldest illegitimate son of Charles II, born to his mistress Lucy Walter, landed at Lyme Regis with just 82 followers, hoping to rally Protestants to his cause and depose his uncle. It didn't happen. Although Monmouth gathered some support in the West Country, the Monmouth Rebellion ended in abject failure at the Battle of Sedgemoor in Somerset on 6 July 1685, where the Duke's largely peasant army was defeated by the better-led and trained government regulars. Hundreds of Monmouth's followers were sent to trial at the so-called 'Bloody Assizes' under the stewardship of the Protestant Judge Jeffreys. Hundreds were subsequently hanged, or hanged, drawn and quartered, their remains publicly displayed, and hundreds more were deported to the West Indies. The Bloody Assizes disgusted even some of the King's supporters and Judge Jeffreys became known as 'the hanging judge'. Monmouth himself was captured and, despite Uncle James granting him a personal audience, was beheaded on Tower Hill on 15 July. It is said that Jack Ketch, the executioner, botched the job and it took several blows of the axe to sever poor Monmouth's head from his body. There is also a disputed tale that Monmouth's portrait was painted after his death; if so, he looked surprisingly chipper in it, all things considered.

James had married his first wife, Anne Hyde, in 1660, but she died in 1671. In 1688, James's second wife, the Catholic Mary of Modena, gave birth to a son and heir, James Francis Edward Stuart. The prospect of a Catholic inheriting the Crown was a step too far for many Protestants. Conversations had already taken place between leading Whigs, fearful of 'Popery', and the Protestant Prince William of Orange of the Dutch Republic. William was Charles I's grandson and married to Mary, James II's oldest daughter by Anne Hyde. Protestant Mary had been heir to the throne before the arrival of the new baby boy. Encouraged by William, a group of seven English peers (later, quite seriously, called 'the Immortal Seven'), wrote to the Dutch Prince claiming that 'nineteen parts of twenty people' wanted to change their monarch and inviting William to invade. The claim may or may not have been true, but this letter was, technically, an act of treason. For William, a Catholic Britain, and possibly even a Franco-British alliance, was the last thing the Protestant Netherlands needed; he already planned to invade and simply wanted to make it look as legitimate as possible. What followed was a carefully managed coup d'état. Miraculously slipping past the Royal Navy with his invasion fleet of some 450 ships, William landed, unopposed, with an army of 40,000 troops at Brixham, in Torbay on 5 November 1689. His army was well-equipped and included Dutch, Germans, Swiss, Swedes, Lapps and even 200 or so 'black' people (presumably, slaves) brought over from Dutch plantations in America. Gradually, William marched this huge force across south-west England to London, with bafflingly little resistance apart from a few skirmishes at centres of influence like Wincanton and Reading. Mary of Modena fled to France with her baby, the young Prince of Wales. After some faffing about, James followed. These events secured Torbay's place in history and the following year William and Mary became joint King and Queen. When doing so, WilliamandMary (as I think history should call them) accepted the Declaration of Right, passed by Parliament, which confirmed the arbitrary use of royal power to be illegal and provided the basis for Britain's constitutional monarchy - one of the most important events in British history.

In a nutshell, this was the so-called 'Glorious Revolution' – the last successful invasion of these islands; you can stumble across memorials to it all over the country, sometimes in the oddest places. It changed Britain profoundly. Yet, however popular it may have been, and however important an event it was, WilliamandMary's often allegedly 'bloodless' coup was no less than an invasion by a foreign power which overturned a legitimate monarch. Nor was it bloodless, not least because James still had many supporters - known as 'Jacobites' (*Jacobus* is the Latin form of James) – and they weren't going quietly. To kick things off, a Jacobite Highland army defeated a Government army at Killiekrankie in 1689. Earlier that year, James II landed in Ireland, with assistance from France, and was acknowledged as king in Dublin. Gathering enormous support, James was soon in effective control of most of the country. However, his Irish-French army was decisively beaten by William's forces, first at the Battle of the Boyne on 1 July 1690, then at Aughrim on 12 July, and Ireland was systematically re-conquered. Further dissatisfaction with the succession in the Scottish Highlands also directly led to the Massacre of Glencoe in February 1692, when government soldiers, mainly from the Campbell Clan, treacherously murdered 38 men, women and children of the MacDonalds. More died from exposure in the mountains, having had their homes burned.

This is by no means the final chapter of the story spawned by the Glorious Revolution; the Jacobites would be back. Indeed, tensions between some of the more excitable Catholics and Protestants over the past 300 years or so have had further grim consequences in Britain in modern times.

When Britain got a German king

The last Stuart and a unified kingdom

Queen Mary died of smallpox in 1694 and, in 1702, William died after his horse tripped over a molehill. In a futile and puerile gesture, Jacobites raised a toast to 'the little gentleman in a black velvet waistcoat'. Next in line to the throne after WilliamandMary was Mary's sister, Anne. Despite 15 pregnancies, Anne had no surviving children to succeed her. In 1701, the Act of Settlement passed by the English Parliament ensured that no Catholic should inherit the throne – and when the deposed Catholic King James died that year, the King of France provocatively recognised his son, James Francis Edward Stuart, as 'King of England'. It was the English Parliament, however, that called the shots; and it settled on the 70-year old Sophia of Hanover, Protestant granddaughter of James I (VI), who had married the Elector of Hanover. The Act of Settlement also stipulated that monarchs swore allegiance to the Church of England and were unable to wage war without the consent of Parliament.

Meanwhile, the death of the King of Spain (also in 1701) heralded a crisis in Europe because his successor was Philip, 16-year old grandson of the King of France. This would have seen the French Bourbon dynasty ruling over a grossly inflated realm that included Spain, France, large parts of Italy and the Spanish Netherlands (Belgium). An alliance of Britain and Austria opposed this massive increase in French power – and the result was the 'War of the Spanish Succession'. John Churchill, the Duke of Marlborough, commanding a combined British, Dutch and Austrian army along with Prince Eugene of Savoy, defeated France and her Bavarian ally at the Battle of Blenheim in 1704. This prevented a French invasion of Austria and knocked Bavaria out of the war. In 1706, Marlborough's victory at the Battle of Ramillies was decisive and drove the Franco-Spanish armies out of the Spanish Netherlands. The subsequent treaties of Utrecht in 1713 benefitted Britain commercially as well as territorially; France generously donated major parts of Canada (including Nova Scotia and Newfoundland) whilst Spain parted with Gibraltar and Menorca. A grateful nation gave the Duke of Marlborough an enormous pad in Oxfordshire, Blenheim Palace, by way of a small thank you. Nice work if you can get it.

The English and Scottish parliaments had been negotiating over the proposed union of their countries since the 1690s. The two nations had much in common – not least landmass, language, religion and monarch. Still, many were disinterested, though some in England saw advantages in securing their northern border from possible French invasion. The Scots had not been consulted on the Act of Settlement and could easily have passed the Scottish throne to an unfriendly monarch; indeed, an act of the Scottish Parliament in 1704 threatened to do just that. For Scotland, the advantages of union were primarily economic, though many bitterly opposed the idea nonetheless. In 1705, the English parliament passed the Alien Act, which threatened harsh trade and property restrictions in England and English colonies unless Scotland negotiated terms for union and accepted the Hanoverian succession by Christmas Day. After lengthy discussions, and a bit of bribery (the poet Robert Burns wrote that Scottish MPs were "bought and sold for English gold"), the Act of Union was passed in 1707 by both parliaments and Scotland and England officially became one country. Scotland retained its separate legal system and church, but government, defence, currency, taxation, sovereignty and trade were united. There were still varying degrees of unhappiness, which remains the case more than 300 years after the event.

In 1714, Queen Anne, the last Stuart monarch, died. The Electress Sophia having passed away shortly before that, it was Sophia's son, 54-year old German-speaking George, Elector of Hanover, ahead of dozens of Catholic candidates with a better hereditary claim to the prize – not least the exiled James Stuart – who became King George I. Thus Britain entered a new age with a constitutional Protestant monarch, guaranteed to be independent of Rome, and a united nation. Whatever would happen next?

6 GEORGIAN (OR HANOVERIAN) BRITAIN

The last battle

Failed attempts to restore a Catholic Stuart to the British throne

The Jacobites, those loyal to the deposed James II and his successors, just wouldn't go away. When James died in 1701, support switched to his son, James Francis Edward Stuart, 'the Pretender' (not to be confused with 'The Great Pretender', which was a hit for vocal group 'the Platters' in the 1950s and later covered by Freddie Mercury in 1987. Oh yes!). Notwithstanding the Act of Settlement which put George I on the throne, many Jacobites hoped that James, exiled in France, could somehow become king after Anne died in 1714. Indeed, in Jacobite eyes, James was the rightful king and anyone else was a usurper.

It is a common mistake to view the Jacobite rebellions of the 18th century as a conflict between Scotland and England; as usual, things are not that simple. There was a Jacobite minority throughout Britain, which created a certain climate of conspiracy. Supporters of the Jacobite cause in England could be found among those who simply didn't like the idea of a Hanoverian king, as well as among Catholics. And though the Union of England and Scotland was unpopular with many, the Catholic Stuarts were viewed with suspicion by Protestants on both sides of the border; Scottish Presbyterians would certainly not have welcomed a return to Catholicism. Equally, many Scottish Episcopalians – Protestants – were Jacobites.

In the summer of 1715, there was actually some potential for a Jacobite rebellion in south-west England and Wales. But support for the Stuarts ever gravitated toward Scotland, their original homeland, and it is here that the

Jacobite story resonates to this day – particularly in the Highlands. This might be considered a little ironic given that the Scottish monarchy, which had been a Stuart monarchy since the 14th century, had often been at odds with the Highland chiefs. However, John Erskine, the 6th Earl of Mar, raised the standard for revolt in Braemar during the autumn of 1715, declaring James Francis Edward Stuart King James VIII of Scotland and III of England. Mar was able to raise a substantial military force, estimated to be in the region of 16,000 men, quite quickly. Rebel opinion was divided, however, as to the best course of action thereafter – and some considered the timing of the rebellion premature. Be that as it may, a small rebel army of 3,000 headed into northern England, expecting to gather sympathisers as it marched through Brampton, Appleby, Kendal, Kirkby Lonsdale and Lancaster. However, by the time it arrived in Preston in November, it had only recruited about 1,000 additional men, and a government force stood in its path. The resulting Battle of Preston between 12 and 14 November saw fierce fighting in the streets of the town but, despite numerical superiority, Jacobite recruits gradually drifted away and the remainder eventually surrendered unconditionally to the Government. At the same time, the Battle of Sheriffmuir on 13 November near Dunblane, between Mar's rebels and a government force under the Duke of Argyll, halted the northern Jacobite army – though the battle itself was pretty much a draw. The '15 Rebellion - often known simply as 'the Fifteen' - petered out largely due to the incompetence or lack of purpose of its commanders. Its leaders were sentenced to death (though some staged spectacular escapes) and other supporters were deported to America – though many were also pardoned.

The focus of all the fuss, James 'the Pretender', only landed at Peterhead on 22 December, but by then there was no realistic prospect of success - and by February he was back in France.

Despite that, many believed the Fifteen had been a close-run thing. One consequence was the Government's decision to build a network of roads and bridges throughout Scotland, to make it easier to move troops around. Much of this infrastructure, constructed under the command of General George Wade, is still there. And, ironically, some of it was used to good purpose by later Jacobites.

A smaller rising in 1719, this time sponsored by Spain, resulted in the Battle of Glenshiel – and defeat for the combined Spanish-Jacobite force.

Of more significance than the Fifteen was 'the Forty-Five' – which, yes, you've guessed - was a rising that took place in 1745. This serious insurrection has to be seen in the wider international context of the War of the Austrian Succession (1740-48), in which an alliance that included Austria and Britain was pitched against an alliance that included Prussia, Spain and France. The King of France, Louis XV, had proposed an invasion of Britain in 1744, led by Charles Edward Louis John Casimir Sylvester Maria Stuart, son of James Francis Edward Stuart and grandson of the deposed James II (VII of Scotland). Charles has become known to history, rather sweetly, as 'Bonnie Prince Charlie', or 'the Young Pretender' - to distinguish him from his dad, 'the Old Pretender'. Louis' aim was to at the very least cause some irritation to the House of Hanover – though, if the invasion was successful, a restored Catholic Stuart monarchy would be even better and would take Britain out of the war. However, his plans had to be abandoned because much of the French invasion fleet was wrecked in bad weather. But by this time, Charlie's blood was up. Frustrated, he obtained some modest private backing and set sail anyway with a small force on board two ships,

L'Elisabeth, a 64-gun man-of-war, and *La Doutelle* (or *Le du Teillay*), a 16-gun frigate. Things did not get off to a good start for the rebels; they were confronted by a British man-of-war, HMS Lion, off the coast of Cornwall. In the ensuing exchange of fire, both Lion and L'Elisabeth were so badly damaged they had to return to their respective ports. This cost Charles some 700 troops and most of his arms, which had been on board L'Elisabeth. Still, he carried on regardless and in due course, on 23 July 1745, La Doutelle anchored off the Island of Eriskay on the west coast of Scotland. However, the loss of L'Elisabeth meant that Charlie came ashore with a just handful of companions – later known as 'the Seven Men of Moidart' (because there were seven of them and they landed in the Moidart area of Lochaber). Messages went out to the Highland clans to rendezvous at Glenfinnan on 19 August, but this initially met with little success. Eventually, a force of about 1200 men, including MacDonalds and Camerons, gathered there; the Stuart banner was raised and Prince Charles proclaimed his father as James VIII and III - the rightful king of England, Scotland and Ireland. The rebellion was underway. Avoiding the government troops sent against him, Bonnie Prince Charlie entered Edinburgh on 17 September and installed himself at the Palace of Holyrood – with a loyal government garrison in the castle at the other end of town.

In the early hours of 21 September, the Jacobite army fell upon a government force at Prestonpans, to the east of Edinburgh. The redcoats, many inexperienced and most barely awake, were overwhelmed by the Highlanders in about fifteen minutes. It was an emphatic rebel victory. The Government in London recalled regiments from fighting in France and dispatched 10,000 more troops to the north. Meanwhile, the Jacobite camp argued over what to do next. Charles was keen to swiftly exploit his victory, invade England, topple what he viewed as the illegitimate

Hanoverians and secure his Stuart birthright; others had no interest in England or its crown. But, in the end, a Jacobite army of about 5,500 set off south in early November, taking Carlisle on 14th and reaching Manchester on 28th. Like his father's army 30 years before, Charlie hoped to attract more recruits in England as he went; once again, whilst there was little resistance to the invading army, the number of new Jacobite recruits was disappointing – apart from about 300 volunteers who joined in Manchester.

On 4 December, Charles reached Derby – just 130 miles from London. Legend has it that the government was in a bit of a fankle and that King George II considered packing his bags to return to Germany. But BPC's army did not enjoy unified command. The Prince, confident of French support, was keen to carry on, but there was no sign of help, either from across the Channel, or from English sympathisers. Others did not share Charles' optimism and a council of war decided on retreat. There's a story that the clincher was news that 9,000 regular troops blocked the road to London at Northampton, misinformation fed to the Jacobites by a Government spy, Dudley Bradstreet. In any event, the Jacobite army turned round and went back the way it had come. Maybe the French would have invaded, had the rebels not retreated.

The Prince's army was pursued north by a redcoat army commanded by the Duke of Cumberland, second son of George II. Lord George Murray, the most skilful Jacobite commander, did well to manage the retreat in good order. However, Cumberland's vanguard caught the Jacobite rearguard at Clifton Moor near Penrith and a fierce skirmish, in which the Jacobites came off the best, slowed the Duke down. By 19 December, though, Carlisle had been retaken for the government.

On 17 January, near Falkirk, the Jacobites once again beat a Hanoverian army. But, once again, the command was divided over what to do next. Forces were split to undertake minor tasks until, on 16 April 1746, the whole sorry tale ended with the final and decisive defeat of the Jacobites at the Battle of Culloden, near Inverness. The rebels were tired, hungry and both technically and tactically inferior to the better trained and disciplined Government troops. It was all over in about an hour. Afterwards, Cumberland's soldiers massacred surviving Jacobites, including the wounded; the carnage was appalling, and indiscriminate. These days, Cumberland would have been tried as a war criminal. But it didn't end there. In the months that followed, Government troops ruthlessly terrorised the Highlands, killing, raping, plundering, burning, destroying the means by which people lived. No one knows how many perished in this disgusting 18th century barbarism and attempted ethnic cleansing. Hundreds were deported to the colonies to work on plantations. Cumberland is rightly known to history as 'Butcher'. As part of its counter-insurgency tactics, the Government dismantled the Highland clan system and outlawed tartans, the possession of arms - and bagpipes. Many clan chiefs lost their lands, some lost their heads and some went into exile.

As for Charlie, with a price on his head, he spent six months on the run before making a romantic escape on a French ship. He never saw Scotland again and died an alcoholic in Rome forty years later. Jacobitism would live on as an idealistic notion with some, and a source of heroic tales for many, but would not challenge the British government again. The Stuart monarchy was obsolete.

Authentic Highland culture is said to have perished on the desolate field of Culloden – the last pitched battle on British soil. In fact, the old clan system was already doomed in a changing world, but Culloden accelerated the revolution. One consequence of this inevitable process was the Highland Clearances - an emotive topic, even today, and a complex one. The Highland Clearances is a term that describes the mass emigration of people from their traditional Highland lands and way of life, to the growing urban areas of Britain – like Glasgow – or further afield, to Britain's colonies. The majority of Highlanders had no land rights, so when landlords, including clan chiefs, began investing in sheep farming their tenants were easily dispossessed; entire communities that had existed for hundreds of years simply disappeared. Comparisons can be made with the enclosure of land (consolidating land for more profitable, or efficient, use, often removing ancient common rights in the process) and emparking (creating an estate park, often for hunting by a rich landowner, sometimes involving the eviction of entire villages) that had been going on for centuries south of the border. In the Highlands, some folk were resettled in coastal areas where subsistence farming needed to be supplemented by income from fishing, or kelp smelting. And some Highlanders chose to leave Scotland altogether. Scots had been emigrating to the New World for years to seek a better life: however, during the clearances, they were forcibly evicted from their homes with nowhere to go. There are tales of people being physically herded onto ships taking them to North America or, later, Australia. Some landowners – and the most frequent example given is the Countess of Sutherland and her husband, Lord Stafford – employed brutal, ruthless, methods to clear land. When the kelp industry declined, and when a potato blight hit the Highlands in the 1840s, migration increased. The clearances lasted from the mid-late 18th century until the late 19th century and have left depopulated areas as well as bitterness behind. No one knows exactly how many left the Highlands in this period, but the impact their arrival had on the new countries of the USA, Canada, Australia and New Zealand has been profound, and many of their descendants have retained an acute sense of their heritage.

The Government also pursued a policy of recruiting Highlanders into the army – initially because they were seen as expendable. At least 40,000 Highlanders – perhaps as many as 75,000 - joined the British Army between 1756 and 1815, fighting against the French in North America and Europe, and against American rebels during the American War of Independence. Highland regiments would become fighting elites; one way or another, the descendents of many of those that fought the last battle would help forge an empire.

British expansion

Britain reaches out…

By 1700, the British East India Company, a private enterprise granted a charter by Elizabeth I, was trading from fortified townships at Bombay (Mumbai), Madras (Chennai) and Calcutta (Kolkata). British colonies were thriving in North America and the Caribbean. By the Treaties of Utrecht in 1713-14, which settled the War of the Spanish Succession, Britain gained Newfoundland, Nova Scotia, the Hudson Bay territory, Gibraltar and Menorca.

In 1739, an indecisive war broke out between Britain and Spain over commercial rivalry in South America. It has been called the War of Jenkins' Ear, due to an alleged incident years before, when Spanish authorities boarded a British merchantman and cut off the captain's ear. However, the war merged into a much larger European conflict, the War of the Austrian Succession in 1740, when an alliance that included Prussia, France, Bavaria and Spain challenged Maria Theresa's succession to the Austrian Habsburg crown. Britain – always concerned to limit French power – supported Austria, in concert with the Dutch Republic, Sardinia and Saxony. The war lurched on until 1748, though Britain withdrew the bulk of its forces from continental Europe in 1745 to deal with the French-supported Jacobite rebellion at home. And then came the Seven Years' War (1756-63).

The Seven Years' War evolved from the separate rivalries between Prussia and Austria on the one hand, in which Britain needed to protect the interests of Hanover, and conflicting British and French interests in India and the Americas. It is seen as the first real global conflict, perhaps the first world war, pitching an alliance of Britain, Prussia, Hanover and Portugal against everyone else of any significance (France, Spain, Austria, Russia and Sweden). In

1757, at the Battle of Plassey in Bengal, Colonel Robert Clive's cunning gave the East India Company control over an area larger than Britain. By the 1760s, the British, through the East India Company rather than by any design on the part of His Majesty's Government, were the dominant foreign power in India, pushing out the French. Clive's use of local puppet rulers established a principle – similar to that used by the Romans - which the British would repeat elsewhere. By modern standards, the man known to history as 'Clive of India' seems to have been an unpleasant piece of work, indulging in levels of corruption that exceeded even those generally accepted at the time. When defending his actions in Parliament, the great man replied, "By God, Mr Chairman, at this moment I stand astonished at my own moderation."

The war had not begun well for Britain, with the temporary loss of the Mediterranean island of Menorca, and there was a real prospect of French invasion at home. But 1759 saw a series of spectacular successes, including an allied victory at Minden (Germany), General Wolfe's heroic capture of Quebec from the French and the naval battles at Lagos off the coast of Portugal and Quiberon Bay in Brittany, which ended any prospect of French invasion and firmly established Britain as a leading naval power. 1759 was called *'Annus Mirabilis'* – wonderful year, the year of victories. The Treaty of Paris which concluded hostilities in 1763 made Britain master of most of North America east of the Mississippi, effectively ending any ambitions the French may have had to build an empire there. Britain also regained Menorca, only for it to change hands a couple of more times until it was finally ceded back to Spain in 1802 – ultimately a significant loss for the British tourist industry.

The motivation for countries to gain overseas territories was, not surprisingly, almost always financial gain. Indeed, many of the characters that laid the foundations of the British Empire were entrepreneurs of one sort or another.

Often brave, and invariably ruthless in the pursuit of wealth, some of them operated way outside the law, even as it was then. But by far the most profitable trade was a perfectly legal one - human trafficking and slavery. The plantations of the New World were labour intensive. The labour was provided either by humans torn from their homes in West Africa, shipped across the Atlantic in appalling conditions, degraded and sold - or by those bred in captivity. Along with their freedom, and their families, these people even lost their names and identities. The trade made men rich; slaves were known as 'black ivory'. And Europe was hungry for the fruits of their labours – the sugar, tobacco, coffee and, later, cotton, for example – and these commodities were themselves also immensely profitable. Manufactured goods and textiles were exported from Britain to complete the famous trade triangle – with a profit made on each leg. Spices, tea and textiles were traded with India. As overseas territories grew, so did trade, creating more markets ripe for the products of Britain's new and developing factories.

Of course, individual traders weren't the only ones that grew rich. Ports such as Bristol, Liverpool and Glasgow boomed and it is impossible to ignore the unpleasant, to some inconvenient, fact that their wealth, and that of Britain as a whole, was partly derived from the misery and inhumanity of slave labour. Liverpool, in particular, was slave city, dominating the trade in the latter half of the 18th century. Trade also feeds other industries and suppliers – including transport, construction and the banking and insurance services required to fund and insure the voyages and their valuable cargoes. So the proceeds of trade, including slavery, helped Britain's fledgling financial services industry prosper, built and furnished opulent country houses for the new elite, enabled the construction of public buildings, such as handsome town halls and churches – and helped establish many of Britain's institutions, such as the

British Museum and the National Gallery.

There was nothing new about slavery, of course; it was a barbaric trade that had been practised since time out of mind. The Islamic rulers of North Africa had a taste for white Christian slaves for centuries – often snatched in coastal raids as far afield as Britain, and even Iceland - which lasted well into the 19th century. The Portuguese and Spanish were the first European nations to make African slavery pay, but, aided by African chieftains (who controlled the supply), France, Denmark, Sweden and the Netherlands all used and traded slaves. However, it was Britain that became the most efficient and prosperous slave trading nation. By the 18th century, there were moves to abolish the trade in all European countries – often championed by nonconformists, such as Quakers. Britain eventually abolished the slave trade in its territories in 1807, but the practice of slavery itself was not abolished in the Empire until 1834.

In 1768, a former collier, renamed HMS Endeavour, slipped out of Plymouth harbour. Her talented Captain, James Cook, had instructions to record the transit of Venus from Tahiti. While he was about it, Cook, a master cartographer, charted New Zealand and the east coast of Australia, casually claiming both in the name of His Majesty, King George III. Nobody seemed to mind… Cook made two more voyages of scientific discovery; he was killed by islanders on Hawaii in 1779.

When the French Revolution espoused principles of freedom and equality in 1789, a few sympathetic liberal noises were initially heard in Britain. However, the methods of the French revolutionaries resulted in 17,000 executions and a further 25,000 deaths by other means. France declared itself at war with Britain, and others, in the name of French Republicanism. A genius Corsican artillery officer, Napoleon Bonaparte, delivered the new Republic victory after victory in Europe. Though Captain Horatio

Nelson destroyed the French Mediterranean fleet near the delta of the Nile in 1798, an invasion of Britain was very much a part of Napoleon's strategy. This was thwarted, however, and Britain's position as the world's premier maritime power confirmed, by Nelson's defeat of the French and Spanish fleets at the Battle of Trafalgar on 21 October 1805. Britannia ruled the waves for at least the next hundred years. The Napoleonic Wars rumbled on as Britain harried a French army in Spain and Portugal and Napoleon was forced to retreat from Moscow. A coalition led by Britain's Duke of Wellington and Prussia's Blücher finally ended Napoleon's ambitions at the Battle of Waterloo in 1815. Apparently, Wellington said the battle was "the nearest run thing you ever saw in your life." I like to think Napoleon said something thoughtful and memorable too, like, "Oh, merde!"

The fledgling British Empire was not just an arms-length thing; Ireland was still treated like a colony. In 1800, in an effort to discourage separatist unrest, Parliament passed the Union with Ireland Act, formally joining Great Britain – England, Scotland and Wales – with Ireland. The United Kingdom was born – as was the Union Flag (or Union Jack) – the red cross of St George on a white background (for England), the white diagonal cross or saltire of St Andrew on a blue background (for Scotland) and the red saltire of St Patrick on a white background (Ireland). Wales, a conquered land for centuries, never got a look in. Ireland was a predominantly Roman Catholic country; whilst qualifying Catholics were allowed to vote in elections, Catholics were not permitted to stand as Members of Parliament until 1829. Ireland was a fertile place for nationalists and the so-called 'Irish Question' came to dominate British politics for many years.

Why they don't play cricket (much) in the USA

Britain helps create several of the world's great nations

Although Britain was busy building its global power in the 18th century, it very carelessly managed to lose 13 British colonies on the east coast of mainland North America. The colonies were pretty much self-governing, with white populations of mostly independent-minded farmers that were overwhelmingly British in heritage. By and large, the British government had pursued a policy of 'salutary neglect' toward people it regarded as its own, avoiding the enforcement of legislation that might limit trade, because it believed this would enable the colonies to flourish. Yet the 13 colonies - Connecticut, Delaware, Georgia, Maryland, Massachusetts Bay, New Hampshire, New Jersey, New York, North Carolina, Pennsylvania, Providence Plantations, Rhode Island, South Carolina and Virginia – fought for their independence and ultimately formed the United States. So - what happened?

North America was a primary theatre of operation in the Seven Years War (1756-63), at the end of which all of France's former territories in North America had been ceded to Britain, as well as Florida (from Spain). The wars had been expensive, doubling the national debt, and the new territories involved Britain in additional administrative and military expenses. The government in London introduced a series of clumsy taxes to raise money from all of its colonies, including a tax on sugar in 1764 and a stamp duty in 1765, which caused particular resentment in America, provoking the slogan – "no taxation without representation" (the colonials had no seats in the British Parliament). After furious protests, most of the taxes were repealed – except for a duty on tea.

Some colonists also resented the Royal Proclamation

which declared the lands gained from France to be Crown property and prohibited colonists from settling them. There were, too, radical anti-British voices being raised - after all, many colonists had travelled across the Atlantic to escape the mother country and start afresh. In 1770, British troops opened fire on a mob that had attacked a sentry outside Boston's State House. In 1773, a party of Bostonians, some disguised as native Indians, boarded three ships of the East India Company docked in the harbour laden with tea, and tipped the cargo into the sea – an event that became known as the Boston Tea Party. Britain's reaction to the intended affront to authority was to pass a series of draconian acts, the Intolerable Acts, which included closing the port of Boston – and, not surprisingly, that just made matters worse. Delegates from 12 of the 13 colonies meeting in Philadelphia in 1774 (The First Continental Congress) called for a boycott of British goods.

Armed conflict began in April 1775, when British troops sent to seize stores of gunpowder in Lexington and Concord were confronted by colonial 'minutemen' – militiamen intended to be ready for action in a minute. No one knows who fired the first shot – "the shot heard round the world" (according to Ralph Waldo Emerson) - but 8 colonials were killed at Lexington and 70 British soldiers at Concord. There were conciliatory voices who wanted to reach agreement, but war sometimes carries its own momentum and there was a definite shift toward a break with Britain. The Second Continental Congress created a Continental Army in June 1775, with Virginia Congressman George Washington – who had recently been fighting with the British against the French and native Indians - as its Commander in Chief. The Royal Navy controlled the seas and, to begin with, fortunes on land were mixed for both sides. On 4th July 1776, the colonials declared independence from Britain, which included one of the most ringing passages in the English language:

"We hold these truths to be self-evident, that all men are created equal, that they are endowed by their Creator with certain unalienable Rights, that among these are Life, Liberty and the pursuit of Happiness."

Regrettably, slaves, native Indians and women were exempt. The American War of Independence was not a crusade for universal freedom; Washington himself owned about 300 slaves.

In 1777, an entire British army surrendered at Saratoga, which encouraged France, Spain and Holland to, rather unsportingly, support the rebels. This widening of the war proved decisive; it is debateable whether the Americans could have won alone, without the additional forces ranged against the British. Britain also had problems at home, where the war was unpopular. Any victories it achieved were at a disproportionately high cost in casualties and, in addition, the entire conflict was extremely expensive, financially. The military historian Richard Holmes argued that Britain was in no position to deliver the killer blow needed to defeat the rebels, who only needed to remain a viable fighting force. Interestingly, it has been estimated that about one in five colonials were loyal to Britain and about a third did not want to get involved fighting with either side and pretty much sat on the fence. The population of the 13 colonies was around 2.4 million and the rebels, 'the Patriots', numbered no more than 50% of the population at any one time. Had Britain offered a measure of self-rule at the outset, perhaps war would have been averted and history would have taken a different course.

In any event, the end came at Yorktown in Virginia in October 1781, when Britain's General Cornwallis, besieged by a French fleet, surrendered to a combined rebel/French army under Washington. The war was formally concluded by the treaty of Paris in 1783. Following the war, an estimated 80-100,000 Loyalists left the new United States, about half of them ending up in British North America – Canada, as it is now called.

So, the United States broke away from Great Britain - and they seem to be doing OK without us. It is important to remember that the American War of Independence was not a war between two sovereign states. Indeed, there are elements of a civil war about it. Whatever reasons people had for making the hazardous journey to the New World – economic, religious, political, to escape persecution, or make a fresh start – a majority at that time shared a common British heritage and culture. Some had been born in the old country, while many had parents or grandparents who had been. Even though the UK and the US were to often fall out in the future – not least when British troops occupied Washington and set fire to the White House in 1814 – by and large the two nations have rubbed along fairly well ever since. Would rock 'n' roll have been invented if Britain had won? Maybe not; so perhaps things worked out for the best after all.

One consequence of the new independent United States was that Britain had to stop exporting its unwanted convicts to America – which it had been doing since about 1718. From the 1780s until the 1860s, the main destination for penal transports was Australia. Thus did Britain help create two of the world's great nations…

The 'First Fleet', as it was called, of 11 ships sailed from Portsmouth for Australia on 13 May 1787 under the command of Arthur Phillip. It carried about 790 convicts, including around 190 women and 14 children – though accounts vary. There were roughly the same number of ships' crew, marines and 'others'. The ships arrived in Botany Bay in January 1788. Phillip soon identified Port Jackson as a better location and moved the colony there, where it provided the nucleus for the city of Sydney.

Penal transportation was actually viewed as a more humane alternative to the severe punishments that could be meted out in the 18th and 19th centuries for what today would be considered relatively minor misdeeds. By 1750, 160 offences, including petty theft, carried the death penalty in Britain. The number of capital offences had increased to 288 by 1815 – a series of laws that historians have dubbed 'The Bloody Code'. The relative leniency of transportation was unlikely to be shown to those convicted of serious crimes, like rape or murder, but people could be sentenced to penal servitude for acts that were considered seditious. For example, six men from Tolpuddle in Dorset (the 'Tolpuddle Martyrs') were transported in 1834 for, effectively, forming a trade union. Something like 162,000 convicts were transported to Australia until the practice ended in 1868. The voyage was long – roughly 6 months - the conditions were appalling and some did not survive the trip. At the end of their terms, the majority of prisoners settled in Australia – though some returned to the UK. Incidentally, another option was to sentence men to serve in the army or navy.

Of course, the Australian dimension meant that they have had time to get used to the idea of cricket. Curiously, it doesn't seem to have caught on in quite the same way in the United States – or even Canada. Many believe that the cradle of cricket was on Broadhalfpenny Down, near the village of Hambledon in Hampshire, where Hambledon Cricket Club dominated the game in the late 18th century and where the laws of the modern game developed. The game is older than that – no one knows its precise origins – but it seems to have originated in south-east England. And you might find the Bat & Ball pub opposite Broadhalfpenny Down still serves a good pint.

Britain's industrial revolution

The invention of modern cities and the start of consumerism

Britain was the world's first industrial nation. During the 18th and 19th centuries, a complex series of interdependent factors spontaneously combined over a similar timeframe, which progressively and profoundly altered society, and the environment. They set in motion the Britain of the future: no longer a predominantly rural economy where most people scratched a subsistence living from the land, but an industrial economy where most people lived and worked in towns in return for wages. Many of Britain's largest cities – Birmingham and Manchester, for example - were pretty much non-existent before all this happened, and much of the landscape looked very different too. Gradually, the foundations were laid for today's, largely urban, consumer society.

The complex series of interdependent factors were partly natural and partly a consequence of Britain's history. They included having an abundance of coal, iron - and water; a developing socio-political climate that facilitated the growth of a middle class of entrepreneurs, businessmen, investors and thinkers, free from the shackles of an intellectually retarded and oppressive church; a system of government based on Parliamentary law which did not necessarily favour the narrow interests of an aristocratic elite, or the whims of an autocratic monarch; innovations in agriculture, science, healthcare and transport; and the availability of growing markets at home and overseas in which to sell goods. All of these factors fed into and off one another; you could say that Britain got very lucky.

Industrial growth and social development is impossible if most of the population is working its fingers to the bone simply in order to produce enough food to survive. Those circumstances allow no capacity for innovation. Traditional farming methods in Britain were labour intensive. Medieval peasants tended narrow strips of land - which could often be some distance from one another – to grow crops (evidence of medieval strip farming in modern fields is commonplace today). Livestock could be grazed on common land. It had long been recognised that enclosing land was more efficient and increased production. Enclosures took place in Tudor times, but a series of Enclosure Acts from 1750 created the patchwork of fields bounded by hedges and walls that are familiar in lowland Britain nowadays. Efficiency was further increased by other innovations such as crop rotation, and increasing mechanisation – like Jethro Tull's seed drill (1701). Enclosures and the loss of common grazing rights dispossessed many of land and resources they had traditionally depended upon to live. And because improved agricultural methods increased production, fewer people were needed to work on the land anyway. Not only could the population be better fed, but manpower was released to do other things – including working in mines and factories, to become traders or shopkeepers – and to be consumers. People moved to towns in search of work, a massive uncontrolled migration with profound social consequences.

Great advances in scientific theory and understanding had been made by giants of the renaissance such as Copernicus, Galileo and Kepler - and in 17th century Britain by Newton. Long-held beliefs were being overturned. The world was being explored, revealing more about the life it supported. Crude international travel itself bred innovation – for example, in navigation, trade and organisation. Britain had replaced its absolutist monarch with a constitutional one; anything was possible. Without the limitations of the medieval world, particularly in Protestant countries like Britain and the Netherlands, mankind could dare to believe in the power of reason. All of this contributed to technical innovation - and technical innovation facilitated industrial production.

Traditionally, goods were made in people's homes, often by skilled workers. The introduction of purpose-built factories led to the decline of these cottage industries, and the development of the factory system and mass production. Mechanised production reduced the need for skilled workers. Before industrialisation, wool was king of the textiles in Britain. The first genuine factory was actually a silk throwing mill in Derby, built by Thomas Lombe in 1719. But it was the availability of American cotton (produced by slave labour) and the production of cotton goods that would be at the forefront of the factory system. In 1733, John Kay invented the 'flying shuttle', which enabled a weaver to double previous output. The invention of the 'spinning jenny' by James Hargreaves in 1764 increased the rate of spinning the threads to make the weave – and the spinning jenny could still be used at home. Richard Arkwright collaborated with John Kay to produce a spinning frame, which produced a stronger thread than the jenny, but which was too large to be operated by hand. Arkwright installed it at his Cromford Mill factory in Derbyshire in 1771, running it on the power of water, and where he employed some 300 people; by 1816, his workforce had more than doubled. But, by then, some factories were employing more than 1500 people – the 'dark satanic mills' referred to by William Blake.

A further driver (pun intended) in Britain's industrialisation was the development of the steam engine. A Devon man, Thomas Savery, patented a steam pump in 1698, but it was another native of Devon, Thomas Newcomen, who developed the first really successful piston steam engine, which was in use pumping mines from at least 1712. Then a Scottish instrument maker, James Watt, took the next crucial step. Given a model of Newcomen's engine to repair in 1764, he realised he could make it more efficient. Setting up in partnership with Matthew Boulton in Birmingham in the 1770s, the firm of Boulton & Watt manufactured steam engines to not only pump water from tin and coal mines, but, critically, to also drive equipment in cotton, paper, flour and iron factories. Engines of the type designed by Watt were used to propel boats as early as the 1780s. The next step, the steam locomotive, came in the 19th century.

Steam power would transform transport in Victorian Britain, and all over the world. But before that happened, materials still needed to be moved to and from factories, ports and markets. There were two travel options in the 18th century: overland or over water. Up to the 18th century, the responsibility for road maintenance in Britain rested mainly with local parishes – and the state of roads generally ranged from poor to impossible. From 1707, a number of 'turnpike trusts' were set up, combining a variety of interests (eg parishes, businessmen) to improve highways that crossed several parishes, levying tolls on those that used them. Travel by road got easier, in patches. Better construction methods in the late 18th/early 19th centuries, promoted first by Thomas Telford and then by John McAdam, helped improve matters further. Roads were definitely the preferred choice for passenger transport, thus providing the means by which people migrated; and ideas and news spread more than at any time previously. But whilst roads were fine for shifting relatively small quantities of lightweight goods, sometimes fairly quickly, horse-drawn carriages could not provide an effective means of carrying bulk materials and goods to factories and markets. Water transport, on the other hand, was fine for navigable rivers near ports, but that was no good for inland transport and for easy access to coalfields. The desire over many years to make rivers more navigable created a growing momentum to construct artificial channels – canals – carrying large capacity barges that could be towed by horses. The textbook date for the opening of Britain's canal age is 1761, when the Duke of Bridgewater's canal connected his colliery at Worsley in Lancashire almost to Manchester, and included unprecedented engineering features such as an aqueduct and a tunnel. In fact, canals had been built in Britain before that (and the Chinese built a Grand Canal in the 7th century) but there was a spate of British canal-building between the 1760s and 1830s, creating an unplanned system of waterways which enabled raw materials to be more easily and cheaply moved to the factories that needed them, products to be more easily shipped to and from ports, and growing towns to be fed. The growth of railways from the 1830s, the biggest engineering project in Britain's history, brought canal building to an end, though waterways continued in use as a cheaper and slower system of transport until many fell into disuse, before gaining a new lease of life as a source of leisure and recreation in the latter half of the 20th century.

Ironworking in Britain had long been sited adjacent to sources of ore - and forests, because the smelting process required large quantities of charcoal. In 1709, Abraham Darby in Coalbrookdale, Shropshire, discovered that cast iron could be smelted using coke, a purified product of coal. Just to prove the point, in 1777-79, Darby's grandson (also Abraham) constructed the world's first cast-iron bridge, over the river Severn a little downstream of Coalbrookdale. Meanwhile, in the Hampshire village of Fontley, in 1784, Henry Cort patented the puddling technique of manufacturing wrought iron, as well as introducing a rolling mill to produce bars of iron. Cort's innovations allowed coal to be used for refining and steam power for producing bar, or rolled, iron. The iron industry, no longer dependent on charcoal or water, could be more mobile – though often sited not far from sources of coal. The ability to produce large sheets of iron transformed manufacturing equipment and construction in general. The demand for iron – and steel – as well as the growth of steam power, in turn fuelled (pun intended again) the expansion of coal mining.

The irony of industrialisation is that whilst it was to create amazing wealth for Britain, a developing middle class and, painfully slowly, ultimately a generally higher standard of living, its unplanned nature intensified the poverty in which most people lived whilst it was taking place. Moreover, the concentration of people living in close proximity in urban areas, usually in damp or unsanitary conditions, increased the risk of death by diseases such as typhus, cholera and, the biggest killer of all, tuberculosis. It is astonishing, then, that in parallel with all of this, there was a demographic revolution too. It is estimated that the population of England and Wales in the late 17th century was about 5.5 million. By 1801 this had risen to 9 million - an increase of more than 63% in just over 100 years – plus a further 1.5 million in Scotland. By 1851, the population of Britain was 21 million – an increase of almost 83% in just 50 years (ie an average of about 190,000 additional people each year). This growth was almost entirely organic. It may have been in small part due to medical innovations, such as Edward Jenner's discovery of vaccination against small pox in 1796, and perhaps a greater awareness of health issues and care – though the emergence of a medical profession that was more likely to cure patients than kill them was a very gradual process indeed. Even so, the death-rate fell, the birth-rate rose and there was a significant drop in infant mortality – suggesting improvements in midwifery. A greater understanding of vitamins would eventually help everyone. (British sailors were allegedly called 'limeys' because the Royal Navy recognised that fresh fruit prevented scurvy, a practice championed by our friend Captain Cook). Better building methods and materials would, in time, improve public health as well.

Britain's industrialisation was a remarkable and continuous process through the 19th and into the 20th centuries, forging the physical and social fabric of Britain - and setting in motion the climate of constant change that we now take for granted.

"The greatest happiness of the greatest number"

Britain wakes up to reason

Exploring new lands, making new scientific discoveries, questioning long-held religious doctrines – even getting rid of the odd king or two – all of these things were part of Britain's story between the 16th and 18th centuries. Creative energy, though, was certainly not unique to Britain; there was so much of it bouncing about Europe at this time, challenging the established order and pioneering social reform, that historians have given it a nice label – 'The Enlightenment' – or perhaps more accurately - 'The Age of Reason'. People like labels. Man has progressively challenged physical and intellectual boundaries, but there is no escaping the explosion of thinking that occurred in Europe in the wake of the Reformation and at the end of the Renaissance. Perhaps it was merely a natural continuation, part of Man's evolution, taking place in parallel with an expanding knowledge of the world, an increase in international trade, groundbreaking scientific advances and the industrial revolution.

The Enlightenment is characterised by liberalism, tolerance and scientific questioning as well as opposition to absolutism and religious dogma. Its principles helped inform the American and French revolutions, as well as paving the way for modern western societies. The period of the Enlightenment spanned the 17th to the early 19th centuries, depending (I guess) on personal bias – and it means slightly different things in different countries. Scotland had its very own enlightenment, due to the particular achievements of Scottish philosophers and scientists in the 18th century, but a central and crucial feature of the Age of Reason is its international nature. Was this the first time in history that there was not only an outpouring of intellectual thought, but also the means and the will for this to be communicated between nations so effectively? Ideas only make a difference if they are spread.

Crucial to the spread of ideas, of course, was the growth of literacy. Once upon a time, the ability to read and write was limited to a very few, most of them churchmen. With the invention and spread of printing came the ability to produce a range of written material and, moreover, material in the local language. One consequence of the Reformation in Britain was the production of the Bible in English; so now people could read the Word of God for themselves – an incentive to become literate. Without printing and the growth of literacy there would have been no Enlightenment.

Mentioning just a select few of the luminaries associated with this spontaneous movement, we have: the Englishman John Locke (1632-1704), sometimes known as 'the father of liberalism' and whose words influenced Thomas Jefferson when writing the Declaration of Independence; the genius of Isaac Newton (1642-1726), another Englishman, who published his 'Philosophiæ Naturalis Principia Mathematica' in 1687 and whose laws of motion and gravity underpin so much of modern physics; the Saxon Gottfried Leibniz (1646-1716), who invented binary arithmetic; the hugely influential and multi-talented Frenchman, Voltaire (1694-1778), another influence on the fledgling United States, promoter of freedom and the separation of church and state; David Hume (1711-76), Scottish philosopher, economist and historian; Jean-Jacques Rousseau (1712-78) in Geneva, whose views were so admired by French revolutionaries and who espoused the importance of education; Adam Smith (1723-90), another Scot, whose 'Inquiry into the Nature and Causes of the Wealth of Nations', published in 1776, defined capitalism and has earned him the title 'father of economics'; the Prussian Immanuel Kant (1724-1804), champion of universal peace and international cooperation; Edmund Burke (1729-97), an Irish/British statesman who supported American independence and Catholic emancipation; Thomas Paine (1737-1809), inspirational political thinker from Norfolk, who was convicted of seditious libel in Britain. And not forgetting dear old Jeremy Bentham (1748-1832), the London-born philosopher and reformer quoted in this chapter's title, who asked for his body to be put on display at University College London after his death.

Through their work, this august body of scholars – and more besides - laid the foundations for what we might (or might not) like to call 'modern liberal secular democratic capitalism'. Just think, without them, Britain might be the sort of place where you can't say what you like without someone getting upset about it.

Revolting Britain

Change makes people restless

The radical thinkers of the 18th century offered tantalising visions of a more just society. Their ideas greatly influenced the French and American revolutions, which produced two of the world's great republican democracies. In Britain, the loss of the American colonies was largely accepted with a sense of detached interest, and many reform-minded Britons initially related to and sympathised with the aspirations of the French Revolution. But feelings changed when the Terror began across the Channel and Britain again found itself at war with France. There was real fear of the mob among the ruling classes, as well as of the old bogey-man of Jacobitism. In 1793, Prime Minister William Pitt suspended Habeas Corpus (the right of a person detained by the authorities to have the legality of that detention examined by a court of law) and in 1795 introduced the so-called 'gagging acts' (the Seditious Meetings and the Treason Acts), which restricted public gatherings.

Protests were as much a feature of Britain two or three hundred years ago as they are now, albeit back then they were more spontaneous, and often violent. In 1743, there were riots after repeated government attempts to restrict the sale of gin – excessive gin consumption was an extremely serious risk to health at the time. Riots also broke out amongst the weaving industry in London's Spitalfields: in 1769, soldiers sent to arrest suspected rioters killed two and four were later executed. In Birmingham in 1791, a crowd attacked religious dissenters. The same year, in the small town of Tranent, near Edinburgh, 12 people were killed when soldiers were dispatched to put down a protest against being press-ganged to join the British Army. Back in London, in 1809, there were even riots sparked by an increase in the price of theatre tickets.

But fear of the mob was also based on bitter experience. In 1780, an enormous crowd led by Lord George Gordon marched on the House of Commons to protest against modest measures of Catholic emancipation. The crowd turned into a pack, estimated to be about 60,000 strong, that rampaged through London setting fire to properties belonging to Catholics. The so-called Gordon Rioters went on to attack the Bank of England and various prisons, releasing the inmates of Newgate. Troops were sent in and 200 people died.

During the Napoleonic Wars (1803-15), a combination of low wages, high taxes, unemployment, poor harvests - and consequently food shortages and higher prices - caused considerable unrest and civil disturbance from the south-west to Newcastle. Economic pressure forced many men to sign up for the army, but this often left their wives and children at the risk of destitution at home. Improved mechanisation contributed toward unemployment for some: in the textile industry, for example, new wide-framed looms could be operated by lower-paid unskilled workers. But so-called 'Luddites', thinking to save their jobs, destroyed cotton frames in the north and midlands of England and riots became widespread between 1811 and 1813. The Frame Breaking Act of 1812 created a new capital crime, leading to executions and transportation. (The name 'Luddite' was coined either because their leaders were called after the legendary King Ludd, a mythical founder of London, or from a mysterious Ned Lud who was alleged to have smashed stocking frames in Nottingham in 1779. In any event, nowadays, the term is used to refer to someone who is opposed to technical or industrial advances.)

The Corn Laws, introduced in 1815, imposed a tax on imported wheat to protect domestic production, but forced the price of bread so high that many could not afford to buy it. People were hungry. Discontent was growing –

exacerbated by frustration that, because so few were allowed to vote, Parliament only represented the views of the wealthy self-interested elite. Some 60,000 people attended a peaceful demonstration held in 1819 at St Peter's Fields in Manchester. The crowd gathered to hear Henry Hunt, a leading political reformer, speak about reform. However, alarmed magistrates called in local troops to arrest Hunt and clear the area, which they did by riding into the crowd with sabres drawn. At least 11 demonstrators were killed and some 500 were wounded. The event became known as the Peterloo Massacre, ironically comparing the event at St Peter's with the carnage of the national victory at Waterloo four years earlier. In response, Parliament astonishingly passed 'the Six Acts' which, amongst other things, prevented writings and gatherings considered to be 'seditious' or 'treasonable'. The government later claimed an incident known as the Cato Street Conspiracy, a failed attempt to assassinate the cabinet, justified the Six Acts – though it seems that the Cato Street Conspiracy was at least partially encouraged by an undercover government agent. Five of its leaders were publicly hanged, and then posthumously beheaded; five others were transported for life.

Yet - there was no sudden, violent, political revolution in Britain. The country certainly faced inevitable social revolution, but the shift in the balance of power was a very gradual process.

In 1829, Home Secretary Sir Robert Peel introduced the first regular civilian police force in London - excluding the independent, wealthy, City of London. Its officers became known as 'peelers', or 'bobbies' and they replaced an inadequate system of parish constables and watchmen, augmented by 'Bow Street Runners', an early attempt at policing pioneered by the author Henry Fielding. The new Metropolitan Police was a single force that could maintain public order in a consistent manner based on centrally determined policy, and without the need to call upon troops who were liable to use lethal weapons. 'Peelers' were equipped merely with truncheons, handcuffs and a wooden rattle – and their uniform was intentionally un-military. Centrally funded policing was gradually extended across the rest of Britain, becoming a requirement in 1856.

How Britain got the vote

When we got to exercise our franchise

Britons can be hopelessly optimistic, but paradoxically also fairly cynical, about Parliament and politicians. There's nothing new about incompetent, or even dodgy, politicians and, though it may be hard to believe, things could be a lot worse. In the 18th and early 19th centuries, Parliament was particularly corrupt and unrepresentative. The franchise was based on a variety of, sometimes obscure, property qualifications, which meant that most people could not vote; and some constituencies – known as 'rotten boroughs' – had very few voters living in them anyway. Most famously, Old Sarum in Wiltshire had no resident voters at all, but still managed to return two Members of Parliament to Westminster, because the landowner controlled the votes of absent tenants. 'Pocket boroughs' were constituencies that were in the effective 'pocket' of a local landowner and whose Member of Parliament did as he was told. In contrast, the growing urban areas of Britain – such as Leeds – had no representation whatsoever. Parliamentary seats could actually be bought: imagine – that would be almost like a large organisation – a business, or trades union, for example - pumping money into a political party in return for its interests being represented in the House of Commons; why, it's unthinkable!

In the early 19th century, the topic of parliamentary reform was in the air, talked about in the streets and in newspapers like the Manchester Guardian and the Scotsman. Championed by radicals, such as Henry Hunt and journalist William Cobbett, many actually saw reform as just a matter of time, though die-hard conservatives resisted due to a combination of vested interest and fear of mob rule. A Whig (forerunners of the Liberal Party) government assumed office in 1830, headed by a 66-year-old aristocrat,

Earl Grey, committed to reform and bergamot-flavoured tea. The Tory party, forerunners of the Conservative Party, was split between the intransigent 'ultras' and the more modern reformers. A reform bill was introduced by liberal Lord John Russell: it would remove rotten boroughs, modestly extend the franchise from 366,000 to 650,000 and ensure that the great industrial cities of Leeds, Birmingham and Manchester were represented in parliament for the first time. The bill was narrowly defeated by the ultra Tories. Grey resigned and called a single-issue election. In 1831, the bill was reintroduced; it passed in the Commons but was rejected by the Lords. Riots broke out in London, Birmingham, Derby, Nottingham, Leicester, Yeovil, Sherborne, Exeter and Bristol. Rumours swept the land; would violent revolution come to Britain, after all, just as it had in France a generation earlier? When the bill was rejected for a second time by the Lords, Grey demanded that the King, William IV, create enough peers to see it through. The King refused; Grey resigned (again); the King asked the Tory Duke of Wellington, hero and victor of Waterloo, to form a government; but the Iron Duke knew he could not and advised the King to give in. Faced with the prospect of unwanted reformist peers, the Lords submitted to the inevitable and the great Reform Act became law on 7 June 1832. This was a truly historic moment in Britain's story; its political elite had taken a significant step toward redistributing power. Wellington is said to have ruefully remarked of the first reformed parliament, "I never saw so many shocking bad hats in my life."

Yet, despite all the fuss, the 1832 Reform Act enfranchised less than 5% of the population. There was still a property qualification of £10 – a hideously large amount of money for most people in those days – and, of course, women could not vote at all; so the vast majority were still disenfranchised. Even so, Pandora's Box had been opened. The campaign for universal male (and sometimes female) suffrage gathered pace through the 1840s – notably led by the 'Chartists' (supporters of the People's Charter, drawn up in 1838). The 2nd Reform act of 1867 enfranchised all male householders - roughly doubling the electorate from one to two million men – and after the 3rd Reform Act in 1884 it is reckoned that more than 50% of British men had the vote. Wow. Meanwhile, the Ballot Act of 1872 introduced the essential democratic element of the secret ballot.

It was still all about property, though, and it was 1918 before the Representation of the People Act removed all financial constraints and gave the vote to every male over the age of 21 with a residence. Finally, women were enfranchised at the same time – but only those over 30. By 1928, however, it was recognised that younger women could be just as daft as everyone else and universal suffrage for everyone over the age of 21 (with the usual exceptions, such as the insane, convicted criminals and the monarch) was eventually won.

Many westernised countries followed a similarly sluggish pattern, though the German Empire granted universal male suffrage as early as 1871. New Zealand was actually the first country in the world to allow women the vote in 1893 (though some had it on the Isle of Man as early as 1881); in contrast, French women had to wait until 1944 before they got the vote.

In 1969, the voting age in Britain was reduced to 18. Despite all the effort over the years, however, millions of people actually choose not to vote. Turnout at UK general elections between 1922 and 1997 was above 71% - over 80% in 1950 and 1951. In the five general elections between 2001 and 2017, turnout was under 70%. In 2001, 40.6% of the electorate did not bother to vote.

7 VICTORIAN BRITAIN

Wasn't the Victorian era great?

And its legacies are all around us

At 6am on 20 June 1837, in Kensington Palace, London, eighteen-year-old Princess Alexandrina Victoria was woken by her mother, Princess Victoria of Saxe-Coburg-Saalfeld, to be told that the Archbishop of Canterbury and the Lord Chamberlain wished to see her. Pulling on a dressing-gown, the young princess saw the two men alone in her sitting-room. They told her that her uncle, King William IV, had died earlier that morning and that, consequently, she was now Queen. So began the 63-year reign of a tiny (she was barely 5 feet tall), lively and intelligent young woman who would lend her name to an entire era. And what an era it was.

For most of us, Victorian Britain was the land of our great and great-great-grandparents. It was a country that changed more drastically in their lifetimes than over any previous period. The pre-industrial hierarchical society was being gradually nudged aside, to be replaced by a new one in which, by the time the old Queen died in 1901, we can see something of ourselves. In 1901, for example, our ancestors would recognise the term 'public opinion' and take it seriously. Although far from being a property-owning meritocracy, the principles and aspirations of today were being laid in irregular instalments during Victoria's reign. In 1873, all land in Britain was owned by just 4.5% of the population (that is to say that 95.5% owned nothing); in the early 21st century, 70% of the population at least has a stake in their own land - though the vast majority of land is still owned by a tiny minority (but that's another story).

One of the most obvious changes that took place in

Victorian times was the stupendous rate of urban growth, accompanied by a dramatic increase in overall population. Between 1801 and 1901, the population of Great Britain grew from 10.69 million to 37.09 million (15.9 to 41.54 million for the United Kingdom, including Ireland). Britain's towns and cities spread, swallowing up surrounding villages and countryside. Birmingham grew from 71,000 people in 1801 to 760,000 a century later; Glasgow from 77,000 to 904,000. It was a similar story for every major industrial area, such as Liverpool and Manchester. Whilst Britain's older cathedral cities, like Norwich and York, expanded too, the pace of growth there was nowhere near as great. Looking at a map of London published in 1822, places like Kilburn and Hackney are still villages; by 1876 they have been engulfed. London grew from a population of 1.117 million to 6.586 million between 1801 and 1901.

The economic and social revolution that had begun in the previous century accelerated with the coming of the railways in the 1830s and the 'railway mania' of the 1840s, when thousands of miles of track were laid. By the end of the century, 18,680 miles of track facilitated the movement of goods and people to and from every corner of the land (railway tracks peaked at 20,265 miles in 1930). Some towns grew round railway stations, just as others before them had flourished around river crossings.

It wasn't only railways (and railway stations) that changed people and the landscape. The Victorians embraced and exploited new technology and new techniques. Steam power revolutionised farm and factory production as well as transport. Under the direction of a new breed of engineers, great feats of engineering were undertaken - like constructing London's Embankment, enormous sewage systems and the beginnings of the underground railway network. Huge bridges spanned rivers; massive steamships crossed the oceans; docks were rebuilt. The best known engineer of the day is probably Isambard Kingdom Brunel, whose works included the Clifton Suspension Bridge at Bristol, much of the infrastructure of the Great Western Railway – and the world's first iron-hulled propeller driven steamship, the SS Great Britain, launched in 1843. The Victorians largely created today's cityscapes – road layouts, housing, civic buildings, schools... Of course, much of the physical work necessary in construction projects relied on manual labour. And a good deal of that came from Ireland, particularly after the tragedy of the Great Famine of 1845-51. A blight destroyed much of Europe's potato crop. In Ireland, where the potato was the main means of subsistence for the majority of the population, an estimated 1.5 million people died of starvation: many more emigrated – to England, Scotland and further afield, to North America and Australia. As Britain's population soared, Ireland's population actually reduced during Victoria's reign, from about 8 million to around 4.5 million. It is said that 10% of modern Britons have an Irish grandparent.

Britannia had ruled the waves since the Battle of Trafalgar, with the world's most powerful navy, the Royal Navy, protecting the nation's trade routes. Britain managed to avoid the level of serious social unrest that saw monarchies toppled in France, Austria and the Italian states. There was no necessity for war to create or consolidate a unified state as happened in Italy, Germany and the United States. Apart from the Crimean War of 1854-56, Britain also steered clear of European conflicts during Victoria's reign, restricting itself to wars in defence of its opium trade in China, and its Empire in India and Africa, fought against technologically inferior opponents. The Victorian era saw Britain becoming the world's most powerful trading nation, with a massive increase in both imports and exports. Vessels built and registered in Britain dominated the shipping lanes. Asia, Europe and the United States were the principal markets for Britain's exports of textiles, finished manufactured goods, equipment, iron, steel and coal, whilst a booming population increased domestic demand too. In time, Britain's world supremacy would be challenged as other countries – such as Germany and the USA – inevitably caught up.

British goods, design and achievements certainly dominated the world's very first international fair, the Great Exhibition held in Hyde Park in 1851, an event championed by Queen Victoria's husband, Prince Albert of Saxe-Coburg and Gotha. The legacy of the Great Exhibition includes three wonderful institutions - the Natural History, Science and Victoria & Albert museums, partly funded by profits from the Exhibition; it also left us with a south London park and a football team, Crystal Palace (founded in 1905).

Victorian society is seen as highly stratified – a cake-stand with royalty, the aristocracy (including a new industrial elite) and the Church on the top tiers, supported by the professions and a growing commercial middle-class, with the heaving masses on the bottom shelf and, below even that, those that depended on the workhouse for their very survival. The Victorians are also associated with attributes such as duty, thrift – and having a strong moral code that could verge on the ridiculously prudish, like covering up indecent table legs (saucy little things, table legs). Margaret Thatcher reputedly said that "Victorian values were the values when our country became great." Politicians often demonstrate a poor grasp of history. In fact, Victorian values existed cheek-by-jowl with a fair amount of extra-marital fornication and an enormous amount of exploitation. And the prudes tended to come from the growing middle classes - as Baroness Thatcher did. Hypocrisy aside, by and large, the Victorians were also a patriotic lot. It was the height of Empire: got a problem in the world? – dispatch a Royal Navy gunboat to sort it out... What a great time the Victorian era was if you were

British and could afford to enjoy it. Being British was wonderful – the best thing. One can almost imagine our ancestors feeling jolly sorry for all those unfortunate foreigners who happened to be born something or somewhere else. And, even if it might be stretching it a bit to think that they believed God was British, few people would have doubted that English was the first language spoken in Heaven. Perhaps it still is, though it might have an American accent now; perhaps in time it will change to Mandarin, Hindi, or Spanish.

Paradoxically, great wealth coexisted alongside great poverty and hardship in Victorian Britain. But, generally – and perhaps not very obviously if you lived in a Victorian slum or, worse, were consigned to the workhouse – standards of living did actually improve. More goods became available in shops – not only goods and consumables that would once have been produced at home or in the community, but luxuries too - and people were buying them. Everyone, including the working classes, was eating better by the latter half of Victoria's reign; bacon and eggs became common breakfast fare for the middle classes. Though infant mortality was still tragically high, childbirth became easier with the introduction of chloroform. People were living longer too – partly because health treatment was better: Lister pioneered antisepsis in Glasgow, whilst Florence Nightingale (herself, ironically, reputed to be a chronic hypochondriac) gradually helped revolutionise nursing.

There are definite glimpses of the future in our Victorian past. In 1859, Charles Darwin published 'On the Origin of Species by Means of Natural Selection', controversially challenging long-held religious beliefs, and the polymath Herbert Spencer coined the phrase "the survival of the fittest" – an enormously influential concept (and not always a constructive one). The 1880 Education Act made school attendance compulsory. Literacy was growing – as well as an understanding of the world; in 1896 popular journalism was born with the launch of the Daily Mail (by a self-made man, Alfred Harmsworth, who later became Lord Northcliffe). People started taking trips to the seaside (most of Britain's remaining seaside piers are Victorian) such journeys made possible by the new railways that criss-crossed the land. Rail travel, of course, also accelerated the spread of ideas as well as people; Britain was becoming a much smaller place.

Victorian Britain was a dynamic country at all levels; it was a time of restless energy that we might find familiar today. A good number of our institutions, from football and rugby clubs to trade unions (legalised in 1871), libraries, museums, charities and businesses, have their roots in Victorian Britain. Then there's art and literature: J M W Turner, John Constable, Charles Dickens, George Eliot, Thomas Hardy, Bram Stoker, Wilkie Collins, the Brontës, Beatrix Potter, Lewis Carroll, Oscar Wilde, Robert Louis Stevenson, Rudyard Kipling and Arthur Conan Doyle are just some of the Victorians whose works are still universally enjoyed today. Actually, Victorian literature is all over our TVs; the Victorians even, largely, invented our modern Christmas.

It is impossible to avoid the legacy of the Victorians. The Queen-Empress herself lent her name to lakes, parks, roads, and railway stations all over the world and many of us are daily users of the buildings and streets that her subjects constructed. These people helped create our world – and are never that far away from us. If you don't believe me, checkout the local cemetery.

Poor Britain

The squalor of industrial society

Britain experienced the massive socio-economic upheaval that comes with industrialisation before anywhere else in the world. A wealthier Britain was emerging, with expanding middle and urban working classes. It was the birth of the modern consumer society; but there was also widespread and, in places, abject, poverty. It is in fact impossible to overstate the appalling living and working conditions that existed in Britain through the 18th and 19th centuries – and, actually, well into the 20th century too. Overcrowded housing, poor sanitation, pollution, disease, child labour, prostitution and crime were endemic in the growing sprawl of 19th century urban Britain. Though prosperity was indeed spreading, many of those engaged at the sharp end – on the factory floor, in the docks, shipyards and down the mines – lived hard, miserable, unsafe, and often tragically short, lives.

The young German, Friedrich Engels, working in Manchester in the 1840s, was inspired by the "filth, ruin and uninhabitableness, the defiance of all considerations of cleanliness, ventilation, and health" that he witnessed there to write a classic social commentary, 'The Condition of the Working Class in England', which is still in print. This vividly describes what Engels refers to as "Hell upon Earth" the lack of space, the polluted air, piles of rotting material and squalor in "the heart of the second city of England, the first manufacturing city of the world."

Thus were the slums of Britain's major cities, which played their part in developing a modern nation – socially and physically. The unemployed or destitute were often forced to seek refuge in workhouses, funded by local parishes. These were grim institutions where hard menial work was expected in return for survival at just above subsistence level. Many died there and were buried in unmarked paupers' graves, their contribution to Britain unremembered, along with any modest hopes and dreams they may have had the temerity to nurture.

Undoubtedly, most of the problems were caused by ignorance, callous indifference, or a combination of the two. Equally, nobody planned the industrial revolution and all that went with it; there was neither the physical nor organisational infrastructure in place to manage its consequences. Taking one city as an example, Glasgow has a proud cultural history: a university town since the 15th century, it thrived on the tobacco trade, shipbuilding, sugar refining, textiles, brewing and the trade of its merchants. It has fine, often elaborate, Victorian buildings and likes to remind visitors that it was once regarded as 'the second city of the Empire'. Yet its wealth contrasted with the squalor of its slums and the extreme poverty endured by many of its citizens. Between 1801 and 1841, the population of Glasgow almost quadrupled from 77,000 to 287,000. From 1841 to 1881, the increase was more than 50% every two decades. By 1901, Glasgow had grown to a city of 904,000 people – more than eleven times its size a century earlier. Glasgow's slums were by no means unique – London's were among the worst. Other British cities experienced a similar population explosion and you have to ask yourself, frankly, how well our established local authorities would cope with comparable urban growth today.

Dickens featured some of the worst excesses of poverty and injustice in some of his novels – as did other writers. Not everyone in Victorian Britain was callous or indifferent. Thousands of men and women became involved in social work and philanthropy. And not all employers set out to ruthlessly exploit their employees. Enlightened factory owners such as Robert Owen in New Lanark, Titus Salt in Bradford, Joseph Rowntree in York and, later, William Lever at Port Sunlight, showed what could be done with a little thought and humanity.

Welfare and social reform did, gradually and inevitably, take place – though no reliable safety net existed for people until the advent of the Welfare State after 1945. Various Factory Acts were passed from 1802 onwards - the forerunners of modern health and safety legislation. Very slowly, working conditions improved. It wasn't until 1878 that it became illegal to employ children under 10. The 1880 Education Act made elementary education compulsory for all between the ages of 5 and 13, providing a further catalyst for change. The 1848 Public Health Act established local health boards to oversee coordinated water, sewerage and drainage schemes. Successive acts extended the powers of these boards and the Local Government Act of 1888 set out to reform the disparate array of parish, borough and town councils by establishing County and County Borough Councils with specified responsibilities and elected councillors.

In 1875, the Artisans' and Labourers' Dwellings Act gave local authorities powers to buy up, clear and redevelop slum areas, as well as requiring them to re-house inhabitants. Birmingham was the first city to avail itself of the government loan facilities set up by the Act. A similar Act of 1890 greatly extended these provisions and by 1904 some 80 towns had borrowed £4.5 million.

But, the recent ancestors of most Britons had an extremely rough time of it. Try telling that to the kids today; they won't believe you.

The Empire on which the sun never set

Britain, the global superpower

On 22 June 1897, Queen Victoria returned from her Diamond Jubilee parade in London having had a wonderful day. Loyal crowds lined the streets to see their monarch, a tiny plump little old lady clad in black, pass from Buckingham Palace, through Trafalgar Square, The Strand, Fleet Street and up Ludgate Hill to St Paul's, where an outdoor service of thanksgiving was held. The Queen-Empress returned across London Bridge through Bermondsey, cheered and waved at all the way. Her personal message was sent via the modern miracle of telegraphy. "From my heart," she said, "I thank my beloved people. May God bless them." Victoria was thanking her imperial subjects. They lived in five continents, were of every conceivable race, culture and creed and there were almost 400 million of them – an astonishing 25% of the world's population. It fair makes your head spin, doesn't it?

Representatives of Victoria's beloved people attended her 60th Anniversary from every corner of the Empire. There were cavalrymen from Australia, Canadian Hussars, Bengal Lancers, Turkish police from Cyprus, South Africans, Jamaicans, Sikhs, Maori riflemen, Dyaks from Borneo, Chinese from Hong Kong, gunners from Sierra Leone… Rulers and military leaders from other powerful nations came to pay their respects, including Crown Prince Franz Ferdinand of Austria-Hungary (whose murder in 1914 helped trigger the First World War).

The British Empire was the largest empire ever, peaking in size just a short century ago, after the First World War. The international geographical, political, cultural and linguistic legacy of empire is enormous. In Britain itself, it is all around you in architecture, literature, traditions, slang and institutions; it jumps out at you from countless memorials and statues in parks and town centres, and from banners hanging in a thousand parish churches; it is in the people (of course); you can spot it in antique shops or at car boot sales; often, it's there in the way things are done – most notably on ceremonial days. Empire has influenced British policy and international relationships for years and, curiously, still does. Almost all of the 53 member states of The Commonwealth of Nations, formally the British Commonwealth, were once part of the British Empire – some of them home to people whose ancestors came from these islands.

Some aspects of history can make people feel a little uncomfortable, and the British Empire is a prime example of that. However, we must be wary of viewing history out of context and judging only from the bubble of the 21st century. There was no Grand Design to build a British empire. It was as though it had been acquired, as the historian Sir John Seeley famously observed, "in a fit of absence of mind." Yet this is too glib – a self-deprecating remark worthy of Sergeant Wilson of 'Dad's Army' on finding that he has accidentally come by large parts of Africa. The Empire was built on deliberate acts undertaken by men who were often both brave and unscrupulous. Some of them were highly talented; others were probably quite mad. Their actions included piracy, slavery, exploitation and graft. And, however sincere Victorian philanthropists and missionaries might have been in trying to improve the lot of indigenous peoples, at the end of the day the majority of empire-builders were motivated by greed. Ultimately, this benefited Britain – if not some of its imperial subjects. Nor were the benefits equally shared at home – Disraeli observed that Britain was itself "two nations" – and John Stuart Mill reckoned that the Empire was "a vast system of unemployment relief for the upper classes." It is also an uncomfortable fact that so much

British trade in the late 17th and 18th centuries was based on slavery and the misery of other people – and that so few of our ancestors saw anything wrong in that. However, Britain was among the first nations to abolish slavery, and by the time of Victoria's Diamond Jubilee the Empire was a lot bigger and quite a different place. Still, sometimes the Empire could be harsh and unjust; sometimes, whether through incompetence or design, it was cruel; it was certainly racist (though that was not unique to Britain, nor even to Europe) and arrogant (which wasn't a uniquely British trait either); and it could be brutal. Whether it was a 'good thing' or not is obviously a subjective consideration. Though most people now would accept that one country running another against its will is fundamentally wrong, the British Empire is a fact of history - and all Empires tend to be unpopular unless you're on the staff running one. Ruling other people was not unique to Britain, either – other nations guilty on that count include Austria, Denmark, France, the Ottomans, Portugal, Russia, Spain, Sweden and, latecomers, Belgium, Germany, Italy and the USA.

There were two distinct facets to the British Empire: on the one hand, what might be called the 'westernised bit', in a cultural sense – colonised territories with a shared ethnic origin and which were more or less democratic and self-governing, like Canada, Australia and New Zealand. Then there was the rest – conquered lands ranging from India through south Asia, the Middle East and, grabbed during Victoria's reign, large chunks of Africa – ruled autocratically by imperial appointees.

British forces frequently went to war to protect and expand their accidentally acquired Imperial interests – in Afghanistan, China, India, New Zealand, Persia, Burma, the Sudan and South Africa, for example. Despite superior firepower, and the support of the world's most powerful navy (the main policeman of the Empire), victories were not always easily won. But for about 100 years, Britain was largely unchallenged on the world stage. Except for the Crimean War of 1854, in which Britain and France combined to prop up the ailing Ottoman Empire against the Russians, Britain was fortunate to fight no general war with its neighbours or imperial rivals during Victoria's reign. By and large, Her Imperial Majesty's Government was only interested in threats to its own interests – particularly India and the trade routes to it. So as the United States, Italy and Germany forged themselves into great nations through terrible bloody conflicts (in Germany's case at the expense of the Danes, Austrians and French), and as European Alliances were formed toward the end of the 19th century, Britain stood back in so-called 'splendid isolation'. The relative positions and respective attitudes of the major powers of the day, including the British Empire, all went into the cooking pot – along with a host of other choice ingredients – to gently simmer until boiling over in the new, and incredibly violent, 20th century.

8 EDWARDIAN BRITAIN

Fog in Channel - Europe cut off

The calm before the storm?

Edwardian Britain is associated with big hats and house parties for the very rich; a kind of peaceful, sunny, interlude nestling between the dynamism of the Victorian age and the slaughter that was to come. So, what on earth did they all do while they were waiting for the First World War to start? And what difference has it made to modern Britain?

The dawn of the 20th century saw Britain embroiled in an ugly South African conflict, the 2nd Boer War (1899-1902). It came about because foreign gold and diamond prospectors *('uitlanders')* were being given a hard time by the resident Boers, and appealed for Imperial protection. The war did not go well for Britain at first. The Boers, descendents of Dutch colonists (*Boer* is from the Dutch for 'farmer'), very unfairly used their knowledge of the landscape, clever guerrilla tactics and excellent leadership to out-smart and out-fight the British Army. It was only by adopting a ruthless approach, which included burning farms and herding Boer women and children into concentration camps in which 26,000 people – mostly children - perished, that the British military prevailed. Whilst there is little comparison with the work and death camps established by Nazi Germany a generation later, the British camps were squalid and poorly run; people died not as a matter of policy, but due to callous and criminal neglect.

Now, the 'Fog in Channel' heading above is alleged to have been a newspaper headline in Edwardian Britain (though it may date from the 1930s). In any event, it neatly sums up Britain's attitude towards its Continental neighbours – and itself – at the start of the last century.

Some might suggest that the attitude hasn't changed much. But the fact is that Imperial Britain saw itself as essentially a global player, not a European one. However, one significant result of the Boer War experience was that many Britons were surprised to discover that their country was not as universally adored as they had assumed. The outrage expressed by France, Germany, Austria and the USA when news of the South African camps filtered out drove the point home (in fairness, the critics were equally scathing in Britain as well, where the war did not enjoy widespread support anyway). But Britain had no real mates outside the Empire; and, in an increasingly volatile world, that was seen by some as potentially risky.

Corpulent, pleasure-loving Edward VII was 59 when he succeeded his mother, Victoria, to the throne in 1901. He had a huge appetite for almost everything, not least good food and several mistresses. And he helped Britain find an international chum in Europe. Following a state visit to Paris, a city Edward loved and had often played in, Britain and France concluded the 'Entente Cordiale' in 1904. This was not a formal alliance between the old enemies, but more a recognition of respective spheres of influence in the world, and an understanding that the two nations would cooperate more in the future. It would prove to be particularly significant ten years later.

At home, Britain was struggling to come to terms with a more literate and educated population, in which the aspirations of the working class and women were clamouring to be heard. The cost of food was rising, wages remained largely static and there was considerable unemployment. Poverty was an enormous issue. One study, undertaken by Seebohm Rowntree of chocolate fame on the city of York, caused a particular stir when it was published in 1901. It not only described the horrifying conditions in which almost a third of the inhabitants of one English city lived; Rowntree's publication demonstrated that even those in work could not afford to sustain what he called "bare physical efficiency". It caused a sensation. Many found it inexplicable that such conditions could exist at the heart of Empire. Winston Churchill told an audience that the book "fairly made my hair stand on end".

The Liberals won a landslide victory at the General Election in 1906, largely on a platform of free trade and social reform. The reforms included the introduction of free school meals, pensions, health insurance and labour exchanges. It was remarkable, but it was not enough, or fast enough. Moreover, at the same time as funding reform, the Government also committed itself to building the latest Dreadnought battleships to help show Germany who ruled the seas; and that too was a popular policy.

Though Britain even then prided itself on being a haven for other countries' dissidents, there were indications of home-grown revolutionary tendencies as well. Men like Ben Tillett, leader of the London dockers, believed change would only come through direct action. Most, like Labour MP Keir Hardie, took the parliamentary route – though this was hard for working class men, because MPs were not paid until 1911. The new Labour Party, initially allied with the Liberals, returned 29 MPs in 1906 and 42 in the election of 1910. Membership of trades unions rose sharply – it doubled between 1906 and 1914. However, the weapon of the strike, used successfully several times in the latter years of Victoria's reign, began to be used more aggressively, and frequently. There was a wave of industrial unrest in Britain between 1910 and 1914 which hit coal mines, docks, railways and ship building. Troops were mobilised; in Liverpool, two strikers were shot dead.

In 1909, championed by Chancellor of the Exchequer David Lloyd George and his ally Winston Churchill, the government launched its 'People's Budget', which proposed a significant increase in taxation in order to fund social reforms. It was opposed by traditional Conservatives and vetoed by the House of Lords. The result was the Parliament Act of 1911, which removed the right of the House of Lords to veto any money bills – a significant change that remains in force to this day. It was only passed when the new King, George V, was persuaded to threaten the creation of enough new Liberal lords to overturn the Conservative majority.

And what about women? A campaign for women's suffrage had been going on for decades, but although some concessions to women's rights had been made they were no nearer to getting the vote. Emmeline Pankhurst established a radical wing of the women's movement in 1903. The 'Suffragettes', as they became known, set about raising awareness by committing acts of vandalism and violence, chaining themselves to railings and so on. It got the headlines alright. Suffragettes were imprisoned, went on hunger strike, were force-fed and generally abused. Emily Davison achieved martyrdom when she threw herself under the King's horse at the Epsom Derby in 1913; but women still didn't get the vote.

In 1912, tragedy struck twice beyond these shores when Captain Robert Falcon Scott's party perished on its return from the South Pole and when the largest ship built up to that time, the allegedly unsinkable RMS Titanic, sank on its maiden voyage to New York with the loss of 1500 lives, after hitting an iceberg in the North Atlantic.

Then there was 'The Irish Question'. The issue of Irish Home Rule had been at the forefront of British politics for decades. The Liberal Government was supported at various times by Irish Nationalist MPs; and they expected a *quid pro quo*. In 1914 they got it; a Home Rule Act established a very limited form of self-government for Ireland. But this provoked a furious response from the staunchly Unionist Protestant north, where some 100,000 men of the Ulster Volunteer Force prepared to fight. It seemed likely that a large section of the British Army sympathised with them, and might even refuse to put down the impending rebellion. So much for the idea that Edwardian Britain was a peaceful interlude. In the summer of 1914, Britain was on the very brink of civil war when a much bigger drama began to unfold in Europe.

How did the First World War happen?

Or - how Europe went mad

The First World War, 'Great War' or 'War to end all wars', was the largest conflict on the planet until the Second World War twenty years later. It lasted a little over four years and killed in the region of 16.5 million people, almost half of them civilians. That's around 10,770 deaths each day. Millions more were permanently injured or otherwise affected by it for the rest of their lives. When it was all over, the world was a very different place. Here is an explanation as to how this awful conflict started, and why on earth Britain got involved.

The steps leading to a general war in 1914 could be summarised under five key headings:

1. European rivalries and alliances;
2. Geography and German war strategy;
3. The assassination of the heir to the Austro-Hungarian throne by Serbian terrorists;
4. Austria's reaction to that assassination and Germany's unconditional support for Austria;
5. Callous dim-witted bull-headedness.

European rivalries and alliances

Volumes have been written about the complex and subtle international relationships, rivalries and alliances that helped set the stage for war in 1914. The, predominantly European, world of the time was a simmering cauldron of aspirations, resentments and fears, heavily spiced with unprecedented technological and social change, which could boil over if one of the principal chefs got too upset.

Much is made of the arms race between Britain and Germany in the years leading up to the war. Germany was determined to rival the Royal Navy, which was the largest navy in the world. Both countries, with considerable support from their respective populations, built more ships. It has been argued that German militarism was seen as an increasing threat to the Empire. "We'll have to shape up to these Germans sometime", people said. The popular villains in British novels at the time were often dastardly cunning German spies – or, at the very least, shady central European revolutionaries with beards. Tension was in the air. Then there is the personality of the German Emperor, Kaiser Wilhelm II who, it is said, was insanely jealous of his British cousins, their Empire and Navy, and who wanted his share of world action. That Wilhelm was slightly peculiar and had a disturbed childhood is probably true – though this would not in itself have caused war.

In fact, all of the European nations, to one extent or another, had issues with one another. Anglo-German naval and commercial rivalry; Austro-Russian differences over the Balkans; Russian-German belief in the inevitability of a struggle between Teuton and Slav; Franco-German animosity; almost everyone's concern and shared interests in the ailing Ottoman-Turkish Empire. There is a view that war would break out *somewhere*; it was just a question of who would fight whom, and when. Britain and France had a serious falling-out at a place called Fashoda on the Nile in 1898. And, despite Germany's obvious militarism, the arms race with Britain and the reciprocal feeling that a reckoning was not far away, there was considerable mutual admiration as well. History is rarely black and white. Europeans were also closely tied through culture, trade, manufacturing interdependence – and virtually all heads of state were related to one another by marriage.

So many fingers have pointed at Germany - thrusting, socially advanced and economically strong. It was also a relatively new country, forged into unity from 30-odd disparate states just a generation earlier. The architect of this unification was the remarkable Count Otto von

Bismarck, Chancellor of Prussia, one of the larger Germanic kingdoms. Bismarck's goal of creating a Germany under Prussian supremacy was achieved through warfare - with Denmark (1864), Austria (1866) and France (1870). The Franco-Prussian War was a particularly degrading defeat for France and included the annexation of the predominantly German-speaking parts of two disputed provinces, Alsace and Lorraine (famous, respectively, for large dogs and egg tarts) to the new German state. Bismarck was pragmatic as well as extremely smart: having achieved his objective – a unified Germany – he simply wanted to protect it. French humiliation and resentment, coupled with ancient rivalries, would always pose a threat. Bismarck was also concerned that Germany's geographical position in the middle of Europe put it at risk of a war on two fronts. However, the recently defeated, but culturally close, Austro-Hungarian Empire could be a useful ally – better that than a potential foe. So in 1879 an alliance was signed, with a mutual undertaking of aid in the event of attack by another country. Italy, herself recently unified, joined in 1882 – making it the 'Triple Alliance'. Seeking to isolate France, and also avoid the nightmare prospect of a war on two fronts, Bismarck concluded a 'Reinsurance Treaty' with Russia in 1887. This was not a formal alliance; it was more an understanding to keep on friendly terms.

Unfortunately, Kaiser Wilhelm II dismissed Bismarck in 1890 and allowed the Reinsurance Treaty to lapse. France signed an alliance with Tsarist Russia - as Bismarck had feared - in 1894. The arch republic siding with the absolute autocracy may seem an unlikely pairing, but France and Russia had been growing closer – there was considerable French capital and cultural investment in Russia. This 'Dual Alliance' clearly stipulated that if either party was attacked by any member of the Triple Alliance, its ally would attack the aggressor. From that point on, German fears of encirclement increased, and influenced her military thinking.

Europe's Armed Camps 1914
- Triple Entente
- Triple Alliance

Apart from an alliance with Portugal (since the 14th century), Britain largely stood aside in 'splendid isolation' from events in Europe. British governments were primarily interested in protecting the Empire and global threats, rather than European affairs – though it was felt vital that the balance of power in Europe should be maintained. Nor was Britain, crucially, particularly a military power; it had a relatively small, professional, army, and predominantly relied on its naval supremacy to police its interests. However, with Germany flexing her muscles and the unfavourable international reaction to the Boer War, Britain became interested in making friends. In 1902, an alliance was concluded with Japan, followed by the 'Entente Cordiale' with France in 1904. Though not a formal alliance, the Entente was a significant step and, in 1907, it was enlarged to include Russia – becoming the 'Triple Entente'.

So, a further ingredient was added to the two massive power blocs created by the major continental powers a decade or so earlier. In the middle of the European stage, from the Baltic to the Mediterranean, sat the Triple Alliance of Germany, Austro-Hungary and Italy: straddling it was the Triple Entente - Russia to the east, coupled with France and Britain in the west.

Geography and German war strategy

The Dual Alliance between Russia and France meant that Germany faced the risk of a war on two fronts. All of the powers had war plans: Germany's was called the von Schlieffen Plan, named for the Chief of the German General Staff who first developed it. Von Schlieffen's solution to the problem of potentially fighting two powerful foes simultaneously, one in the east and one in the west, was to aggressively neutralise the weaker one first. Russia, he reasoned, with her vast population and huge size, would be slower to mobilise but more difficult to defeat than France. He calculated that French forces would be concentrated along the shared border, particularly around the 'lost' provinces of Alsace/Lorraine, taken by Germany in the war of 1870-71. So von Schlieffen proposed to attack along an easier route, into northern France via neutral Belgium, capturing Paris and defeating France within 6 weeks. German forces could then be concentrated on Russia.

Assassination in Sarajevo – "The shot that rang round the world"

We have spoken of early 20th century Europe as a simmering cauldron of unparalleled socio-economic change, where international relationships were both interdependent and competitive. It was spiced with a liberal sprinkling of nationalism – including on the part of restless minorities. This might sound worrying, but such conditions do not of necessity lead to war. Nor does murder; it is a popular myth that the assassination of Archduke Franz Ferdinand, heir to the Austro-Hungarian throne, by a Serbian terrorist in Sarajevo on 28 June 1914, caused the First World War. There is no evidence to suggest the killing was sponsored by any of the Great Powers, none of which had anything to gain by FF's death; and even if one of them had been behind the act, it did not have to result in a general war.

There was nothing new about terrorism in the Balkans - and Serbia, in particular, is often characterised as something of a rogue state. In 1903, a group of Serbian army officers had horribly butchered their own king and queen. One of the leaders of that crime was an unlovable nationalist fanatic known as 'Apis', who by 1914 was head of Serbian military intelligence and leader of a terrorist group with the melodramatic name of 'the Black Hand'. Many believe that Apis was behind the plot to kill Franz Ferdinand, but there is no proof that the Serbian government *per se* promoted it. Along with Greece, Bulgaria and Romania, Serbia was a nation that emerged in the 19th century from the shrinking Ottoman (Turkish) Empire. After the Balkan Wars of 1912-13, Serbia's military success saw its territory double; but it was land-locked, desperate for its own sea port, ambitious, proud - and potential champion of Serb (and other Slav) minorities living inside its much larger neighbour, the rambling Austro-Hungarian Empire.

Ruled since 1848 by its whiskered and ailing Emperor, Franz Joseph, the Austro-Hungarian Empire sprawled across central Europe, from the Tyrol to Transylvania, and encompassed at least 11 races, including what we would know as Austrians, Serbs, Magyars, Slovenes, Czechs, Croats, Poles, Italians and Ukrainians. It was in many respects a backward land, where minorities were both alienated and repressed. In 1908, it annexed the previously Turkish provinces of Bosnia and Herzegovina, which Serbia coveted and which included a large Serb population. Though reluctantly accepted by Serbia at the time, resentment festered; many in Serbia became increasingly and – violently - anti-Austrian.

But the path leading to Armageddon certainly passed through the Bosnian capital on that fateful, warm, June day in 1914. The Archduke was on an official visit to Sarajevo and no fewer than 7 Serbian nationalist assassins were also in town, waiting to take him out. A bombing was botched and the grand finale was apparently something of a tragic farce, when the royal car took a wrong turn, had to be pushed backwards because it lacked reverse gear (or couldn't turn) and drew up next to where one of the terrorists, Gavrilo Princip, happened to be standing outside a delicatessen with a loaded revolver. Princip fired just two shots; the first to die was Franz Ferdinand's beloved wife, Sophie.

Austrian reaction and the blank cheque

Ironically, Franz Ferdinand would have gone out of his way to avoid war. Throughout Europe, actually, reaction to his violent passing was generally muted, even in Austria. However, seeing an opportunity to sort out their bothersome neighbour, the Austrian government was quick to blame Serbia for the murder. The concern was what Russia's response would be if military action ensued. Russia commanded the largest army in Europe (1.42 million men), saw itself as the defender of Slavs and also backed Serbia militarily. For Austria, the prerequisite for any action was to obtain backing from her powerful ally, Germany. As early as 4 July, the Kaiser had promised Germany's unconditional support – what history has come to call, 'the blank cheque.' It was this undertaking that made a general war almost inevitable. If Austria was attacked by Russia, Germany would be bound under the terms of their alliance to come to her aid. If Germany attacked Russia, France was bound to come to her ally's aid.

After much faffing about, Austria issued Serbia with an ultimatum on 23 July, demanding a response by 5pm on 25th. The terms of the ultimatum were designed to humiliate – though this might not be considered exceptional, because big states routinely bullied smaller ones. In any event, expecting defiance, the Austrians prepared for war. Remarkably, the Serbian reply, submitted just before the deadline, accepted all of the terms of the ultimatum, except for the demand that Austrian police should investigate the murder on Serbian soil, which Serbia requested be referred to the International Tribunal at the Hague. Earlier that afternoon, Serbia mobilised its army as a precaution. On 28 July, Austria Hungary declared war on Serbia and, the following day, the first shells fell on Belgrade.

It was a month since the assassination on 28 June. On that day, as a Royal Navy squadron steamed out of Kiel after being guests of the German Navy at the Kaiser's annual regatta, the British admiral had signalled to their hosts, "Friends in past, and friends for ever."

Given all the rivalries, alliances, posturing and undercurrents, it sometimes seems as though there was something horribly inevitable about the First World War. This is rubbish; war was brought about as a consequence of premeditated decisions made by rational men. The devil, as always, is in the detail, but the first critical decision following the murder of the heir to the throne of Austria Hungary in Sarajevo was an Austrian one: to militarily humiliate Serbia. The second crucial decision was a German one; by giving Austria unconditional support, the Kaiser provided Austrian hawks with the confidence to be as belligerent as they liked, irrespective of what anyone – especially the Russians – might do.

Callous dim-witted bull-headedness

Some may have genuinely believed that an Austro-Serbian war was justified, or could at least be localised. Other voices cautioned that, if Russia supported Serbia against Austrian aggression and Germany, in turn, supported Austria, this would almost certainly bring France into the conflict as Russia's ally – thus a dreadful general European war would ensue as surely as night follows day. And there were some who undoubtedly did little to discourage that awful prospect, seeing it as an opportunity to settle scores. It must be said, too, that the prospect of war was generally popular with many; when it was declared, there were scenes of outright jubilation in London, Paris, Berlin, St Petersburg and Vienna.

It is breathtaking, and frightening, how quickly the European crisis escalated in late July 1914. Everyone began mobilising for war. All potential participants had war plans. Once started, these were difficult to stop. Military leaders were frantic to keep ahead of their likely enemies' preparations. All over Europe, men were being recalled to their regiments and placed on alert. Appeals for reasonableness and proposals for diplomatic negotiations were ignored or rejected. One question that no one knew the answer to was how Britain would react to the unfolding catastrophe. That summer, the British Cabinet was more concerned about the likelihood of civil war in Ireland than it was about the possibility of a European conflict. On 23 July, the same day that Austria issued its outrageous ultimatum to Serbia, Chancellor of the Exchequer, David Lloyd George, told the House of Commons that relations with Germany were better than they had been for some years. A mere fortnight later, the two countries were at war.

On 24 July, Russia partially mobilised, secretly. The next day, the first German warship steamed through the newly widened Kiel Canal – the Kaiser's shortcut into the North Sea - and thereby into the English Channel. That afternoon, Serbia mobilised – but also submitted its conciliatory response to Austria's demands. On 27 July, Russia's Tsar Nicholas II proposed negotiations, which Austria Hungary did not want. Britain proposed an international conference, an idea rejected by Germany. On 28 July, Austria Hungary declared war on Serbia and the British Ambassador in Vienna warned London that the Austrians were "wild with joy at the prospect." The following day, the bombardment of Belgrade began, the German fleet mobilised and the British fleet was dispatched to its battle stations. Russian troops set off to pre-arranged stations along the border with Austria Hungary. Germany partially mobilised in response. The Tsar appealed personally to his cousin the Kaiser (they were both grandsons of Queen Victoria) to, "do what you can to stop your allies from going too far." On 30 July, Nicholas signed the order for total mobilisation. On 31 July, Belgium and Turkey mobilised.

At 5pm on 1 August, Kaiser Wilhelm ordered full mobilisation and, that same evening, declared war on Russia. That night, German troops entered Luxembourg. The French government ordered general mobilisation. The next day, 2 August, German patrols crossed into France and Germany also demanded free passage through Belgian territory for its armies. On 3 August, the British government ordered general mobilisation, Germany declared war on France and some of her soldiers entered Russian Poland. On Tuesday 4 August, Germany invaded neutral Belgium. Britain issued an ultimatum, demanding the withdrawal of German forces from Belgium. The ultimatum expired at 11pm British time, midnight in Berlin; but there was no reply.

Following the expiry of Britain's ultimatum, telegrams stating, "Commence hostilities against Germany at once" arrived at British military establishments and Royal Navy ships all over the world. And thus Britain went to war.

So why did Britain get involved?

Britain's declaration of war was technically in response to the violation of Belgian neutrality, guaranteed under the Treaty of London (1839) by Britain and Germany's predecessor, Prussia. Until the very last moment, many thought that Britain would not fight. It has been suggested that British indecision encouraged German aggression – though, notwithstanding the global power of the Royal Navy, there were also contemptuous voices raised in Germany regarding Britain's tiny volunteer army. Military conversations had been held between France and Britain, and Britain had undertaken to protect the coast of northern France with the Royal Navy. But though Britain was predisposed to support France, there was no legal obligation to do so. However, no British government could afford to stand aside and allow an aggressive militaristic power to wage war on Britain's doorstep, or to potentially dominate Europe and upset the balance of power. If France, a friend, was defeated, how would British interests be served by having the German Navy stationed along the Channel coast? The prospect could not be tolerated.

9 MODERN BRITAIN

Britain & the First World War

A summary of the conflict and Britain's part in it

The 1914-18 war was a global conflict. British forces, and those of her Imperial Dominions - Australia, New Zealand, Canada, Newfoundland and South Africa, as well as India - fought in Africa, Italy, the Middle East, Salonika (Greece) and Gallipoli (Turkey), in addition to on the Western Front (northern France/south-west Belgium) and, of course, on the high seas. But it was predominantly a land war and the outcome was always going to be determined by whoever won in Europe. Britain had no direct involvement in the fighting on the vast Eastern Front, where the Russians engaged the Germans in staggering numbers in the north and, with their Serbian allies, the Austro-Hungarians in the Balkans.

The German armies that invaded Belgium and France in August 1914 largely overwhelmed all opposition, including the tiny, but highly professional, British Expeditionary Force that had been dispatched across the Channel. With Paris under threat, a French-led counter-attack pushed the Germans back, both sides dug in and a stalemate was reached with a line of trenches stretching 450 miles from Nieuport on the Channel coast to the Swiss border. The line varied little over the next four years, during which time neither side decisively broke the other's defences until the final year. The names of the battles – Mons, Ypres, the Somme (in which 20,000 British troops died on the first day), Vimy, Passchendaele, Verdun – resonate to this day.

Trench warfare was an appalling experience for all sides. Men lived and fought in a network of defensive positions that grew ever more sophisticated. Everybody was plagued by lice; trench foot was endemic; keeping reasonably clean was impossible and performing basic human functions like going to the toilet was unpleasant, and often dangerous. Artillery and machine guns ruled supreme; attacks made in repeated attempts to break the stalemate were preceded by massive and terrifying bombardments, and even the setting of high-explosive mines laid in excavated tunnels deep beneath enemy positions. Infantry 'going over the top' (of trenches) were mown down by machine gun fire like corn by a scythe before many men even reached the entanglements of barbed wire that lay in front of enemy positions. Over time, entire villages ceased to exist, shell holes joined up and the landscape became a featureless, alien, world of mud, slime and the detritus of war. Men disappeared – literally blown to pieces, drowned in mud, buried alive or simply missing somewhere in the no man's land between opposing trench systems. Poison gas, tanks, aircraft and flamethrowers introduced just a few more new and ingenious ways of killing or maiming people. Sometimes, fighting was hand to hand, and medieval in nature, involving the use of bayonets, knives, cudgels, knuckledusters and even spades. The dead were close neighbours, often forming part of a trench wall - or were suddenly disinterred by high explosive. This experience of trench warfare induced almost unbearable levels of stress leading to many cases of 'shellshock', or what today we would call 'post-traumatic stress disorder' (PTSD). If their condition was acknowledged and not regarded as a form of shirking, the lucky ones got 'the talking cure' – psychotherapy was in its infancy; others were treated with experimental electroconvulsive therapy or other untried treatments. 306 British and Dominion soldiers were executed for cowardice. Many survivors suffered nightmares for the rest of their lives. And conditions for the British are thought to have been better than those endured by the French or Germans.

People speak of a 'lost generation' dying in the mud and filth of northern France. That's not quite true, though casualties were certainly enormous and horrendous. The British Empire and its Dominions eventually fielded armed forces totalling about 8.7 million for the whole war, in all theatres, of which about a million died. Germany, Russia, France and Austria-Hungary lost even more (roughly 1.8, 1.7, 1.4 and 1.3 million respectively). British losses were in the region of 886,000, of which almost 17,000 were civilians. But losses were disproportionate: for example, in the British Army on the Western Front, junior officers had a pretty low chance of survival; some of these youngsters, barely out of their teens, many of them products of public schools and universities, would have formed the next generation of leaders. In the wave of enthusiasm for joining up at the outbreak of war, many from the same factory, street or club enlisted together. Because it was considered good for morale, the so-called 'Pals Battalions' kept these men side-by-side – so they trained together, fought together – and died together. Thus the impact on a community could be considerable. But the legacy of 'never again', which so influenced British and French policy in the 1930s, was as much a reaction to the manner of the deaths as much as it was the brutal numbers.

The lovely medieval cloth town of Ypres, in Belgium, has been completely rebuilt since the war, and is almost like a little piece of Britain overseas. The memorial to the missing at the Menin Gate, where the troops used to march up to the front, records 54,896 British and Imperial servicemen whose bodies were never found or identified. It's hard to imagine – think of it as a fairly good crowd at Old Trafford. Running out of space, a further 34,984 names are recorded at Tyne Cot Cemetery just up the road. So - that's almost 90,000 men who, so far as their wives, sweethearts and parents were concerned, simply disappeared off the face of the earth. Remember this is in one small sector of the war, and on just one side of the conflict. Those figures also exclude French, Belgian, Portuguese and other allies, as well as New Zealanders and Newfoundlanders. Tyne Cot is the largest Commonwealth War Grave in the world and contains almost 12,000 burials – including some German. Like many cemeteries in Belgium and northern France, it is located at the scene of fighting. The Thiepval Memorial on the Somme records just over 72,000 officers and men from the United Kingdom and South Africa who died in that sector, 90% of them between July and November 1916, and who have no known grave. Overall, a little over 524,800 British Empire service personnel have no known grave – a staggering and disgusting statistic.

Given the pre-war naval arms race between Germany and Britain, it is perhaps surprising that there was only one really major naval engagement in the whole war, the Battle of Jutland in 1916. Both sides claimed it as a victory, though the Royal Navy lost more ships than the Germans did. But this was the one and only time the German Grand Fleet ventured out of port until the war ended. The role of the Royal Navy was decisive in keeping the German Fleet bottled up – and in maintaining a trade blockade on Germany. This is more controversial; less obvious than the unrestricted submarine warfare conducted by the Germans (which was ultimately beaten by the convoy system), the British blockade was just as brutal, more effective and a deliberate form of social warfare.

By 1917, Russia was on her knees, in revolutionary turmoil and the new Bolshevik government asked the Germans for peace. The French army, bled by its defence of the city of Verdun, had mutinied. The United States of America had declared war on Germany in April, partly because of the German policy of unrestricted submarine (U-boat) warfare and partly because the Germans foolishly sent the Mexican government a telegram in which they suggested Mexico could have Texas, New Mexico and Arizona in return for support in a war against the US. The (Zimmerman) telegram was intercepted by British intelligence who promptly gave the gen to the Americans. Interestingly, the USA was 'an associate power' of France and Britain's – never an ally – which meant that there was no single command structure as there would be in the Second World War.

The Germans launched a massive offensive in March 1918. Using new storm trooper tactics and with numbers swelled by soldiers switched from the Eastern front, they broke the British and French lines and drove the Allies back. The Germans were in a hurry; they gambled on victory before the United States could fully deploy its troops and bring huge material resources to bear that would make German defeat inevitable. By the summer, the offensive ran out of steam and came up against more organised opposition. The Allies counter-attacked, forcing the Germans to retreat beyond their original starting point. Broken economically, militarily, and facing revolution, the Germans sought an armistice. The guns finally fell silent on the Western Front at 1100 hours on 11 November (the 11th hour of the 11th day of the 11th month) 1918.

The legacy of 1914-18

The consequences of the First World War are still with us

The First World War transformed the world forever. The conflict itself resonated through the remainder of the 20th century and set events in motion that have informed the world we live in today. Some of the consequences were obvious at the time - the map of the world, for example, looked very different from four years earlier, particularly after the victorious allies had finished tinkering with it.

The pace of social change accelerated in most places. In Britain, women had taken on many jobs whilst their men were away fighting, would go on to achieve the vote and, eventually, a more equal place in society. The rigid class system was challenged by an enlarged franchise, new attitudes and opportunities - and by virtue of the fact that the war threw men of different backgrounds together to a degree that had never really happened before. And through the 1920s and 30s large country estates began their inexorable decline as their owners could no longer afford the upkeep, pay the increasingly crippling levels of taxation – or perhaps they had lost their heirs in the mud and slaughter of France and Belgium. Domestic service, in which 1.3 million had been employed in 1901, gradually began its decline, eventually ceasing to be normal after another great war (there were still a million employed in domestic service in 1931). A further consequence of the war was that a good proportion of the population was actually healthier and better fed – partly because the government had a vested interest in the welfare of its citizens during the war. The provision of canteen facilities at munitions factories, for example (largely government sponsored), was a practice that was continued by many employers in peacetime.

British Summer Time, introduced in 1916 to help

productivity, and British licensing hours (introduced for a similar reason) are two quirks that remain with us – though the licensing hours have been greatly relaxed in the 21st century.

Conflict often acts as a catalyst for the seemingly relentless drive of technology, and the First World War certainly did that. Not all advances had purely military applications: improvements in powered flight, for example, came to revolutionise global communications and travel. In 1919, 10 years after Bleriot flew across the English Channel, Alcock and Brown crossed the Atlantic and regular passenger services began between London and Paris. Medical developments – such as the first tentative forays into modern reconstructive surgery and psychoanalysis – paved the way for more progressive treatments.

The economic cost of the war was enormous. All of the major combatants were hugely in debt – with the exception of the USA. Inflation dramatically increased the cost of living - most famously in Weimar Germany, where hyperinflation meant that, by December 1923, a loaf of bread cost 428 billion marks (probably at least 428 billion Euros in today's money.) The First World War abruptly ended a period of relative economic prosperity for many, replacing it with two decades of relative economic misery - though the employed middle class was largely immune to this. Britain wasn't economically destitute at the end of war, but was forced to sell overseas assets, exports were massively down and unemployment was at around the million mark for all of the 1920s, rising to 3 million in the early 30s.

The war caused a profound upheaval in the international balance of power. Of the five Empires that went to war, only one, the British, remained intact when it was all over. Germany was exhausted, its population starved by the Royal Navy's blockade, its Kaiser in exile in Holland and its fledgling republic at risk of social unrest, or worse. The

Austro-Hungarian Empire, heir to the ancient Holy Roman Empire, had collapsed and the Ottoman Empire of more than 600 years lay in tatters. The Russian Empire had gone too, replaced by the world's first communist state, the Tsar and his family murdered – and the seeds of tension and mistrust immediately grew between two opposing philosophies – communist totalitarianism and developing democratic capitalism. Huge areas of northern France and Belgium lay devastated; France had been brought almost to her knees by the war. French and British overseas interests actually grew as a consequence of redistributing defeated nations' territories, particularly in the Middle East and Africa. But Britain's Dominions had found increased confidence and cracks were beginning to show in the Empire on which the sun never set. Apart from its human losses, the United States emerged relatively unscathed and, if it had not been obvious before, was now clearly the industrial and economic power to be reckoned with. The shift in the balance of power together with the various peace settlements ironically helped set the scene for most of the 20th century's future conflicts.

The victors' approach to peace was a curious mixture of idealism, self-interest and lack of foresight. The principle of 'self determination', which should have resulted in nice neat countries all containing people of compatible cultures living together in joyful harmony, actually produced some rather strange anomalies – especially in the former lands of the Austro-Hungarian and Ottoman Empires. And France and Britain were perfectly happy to ignore the principle when it suited them; Britain, for example, added 13 million people to its sphere of influence, which included gaining a mandate over Palestine, Jordan and Mesopotamia (Iraq). Britain had also demonstrated either incompetence or dishonesty – possibly both – in promising Arab control of Palestine in return for military assistance against the Turks, whilst in the Balfour Declaration of 1917 simultaneously supporting the establishment of a 'national home for the Jewish people' in the same place. The consequences of this, at best uncoordinated, piece of international chicanery obviously remain with us. Rather more honourably, the victorious powers latched onto US President Wilson's proposal for a League of Nations to help resolve future international conflicts. Unfortunately, this august body had even less teeth than its successor, the United Nations, and was considerably weakened by the USA's myopic decision not to join.

Newly independent, and some completely new, European nations emerged – Poland, Finland, Estonia, Latvia, Lithuania, Austria, Hungary, Czechoslovakia (now the separate Czech and Slovak Republics) and Yugoslavia (now the independent states of Serbia, Croatia, Bosnia and Herzegovina, Slovenia, Montenegro, Macedonia and Kosovo).

The Treaty of Versailles concluded between Germany and the Allies, though, was a real corker. Largely driven by a French desire for revenge and the creation of a vanquished, weak, neighbour who could never again invade, Germany not only lost its overseas territories but was also forced to scrap its air force, reduce its army to no more than 100,000 regulars (conscription was prohibited) and to severely limit the size of its navy (eg no ships over 10,000 tons and no submarines). The provinces of Alsace and Lorraine were returned to France, with West Prussia and Pozen going back to the newly independent Poland – leaving East Prussia separated from the rest of the country. German troops were prohibited from the Rhineland, which was to be occupied by Allied troops for 15 years. Then, just to make every German feel really comfortable, Article 231 of the Treaty made it abundantly clear that the war had all been Germany's fault. In view of that, it was only fair to make her pay for it; so huge reparations were levied too. Thus the seeds of resentment, to be inflamed by the rhetoric of a future German leader, Adolf Hitler, were sown. Thought for the day: if they'd finished the First World War properly, then perhaps the Second World War could've been avoided...

Finally – what of the human legacy? There are around 100,000 war memorials in Britain, ensuring that we never forget the young men from our hamlets, villages, towns and shires who perished. The widespread construction of these monuments was a unique occurrence; most of them were built in the 1920s. Death aside, there were 639,000 British ex-soldiers and officers still drawing disability pensions on the eve of the Second World War. That includes 65,000 men whose disabilities were not physical but mental. Some servicemen were so traumatised by their experiences that they spent the rest of their lives in hospital. Some returned to civilian life and suffered recurring nightmares about the war until the day they died. After the war, there was an upsurge in interest in spiritualism across the UK and the Dominions, as many grieving parents, wives and siblings sought to reach out to their dead loved ones – of which more than half a million had no known grave that their relatives could visit. Many war widows never remarried, and many bereaved sweethearts remained spinsters. To these women, their lost men remained forever young, with posed sepia photographs taken in uniform during a brief leave often adorning sideboards until their owners too passed on. The memory of the First World War, and the desire that something like it should never, ever, happen again, was a potent influence on domestic attitudes and foreign policy in the lead up to World War Two. And Britain still formally remembers the sacrifices of 1914-18, and subsequent wars, at 11am on the closest Sunday to the 11 of November every year.

What happened in the 1920s & 1930s?

Inter-war interlude

The writer and journalist Andrew Marr points out that, unlike other eras in the story of Britain, we have no name for the period between the first and second world wars. It's as though it's a kind of interlude sandwiched between two earth-shattering events during which people were recovering from one whilst waiting for the other. Oh – there was the 'roaring twenties', of course; and if you couldn't afford to be involved in that, then you'd be unemployed or in the pub. This was the time our parents, grandparents and great-grandparents grew up in: and they'd tell you a tale or two…

A virulent influenza pandemic from 1918 to 1919 killed even more people than had died in the First World War – estimates vary from 50 to 70 million people worldwide. Worst hit was India, where it is estimated a staggering 16 million souls perished. The first cases in Britain occurred in Glasgow in the spring of 1918 and it is reckoned the final death toll across the country was about 250,000.

The outbreak of the First World War narrowly averted civil war that was about to break out in Ireland (and potentially parts of Britain too) over Irish Home Rule. A clumsy nationalist uprising over Easter in 1916 was (just as clumsily) put down, but the question could not be put off any longer once the war with Germany was over. Irish Sinn Fein nationalists fought a brutal civil war from 1919 to 1921, to which British paramilitary forces, the 'black and tans', responded with equal savagery. An Anglo-Irish Peace treaty created an Irish free state comprising the 26 southern counties within the Empire. This, however, was hugely unpopular and the matter was only settled after a bitter civil war between rival factions of the IRA in 1922 and the eventual creation of an independent republic in the south, with the 6 northern counties of Ulster partitioned off and remaining part of the United Kingdom as Northern Ireland. Britain formally recognised the republic of Eire in 1948.

Further afield, the principle of self-determination espoused by the victorious powers appealed to a growing sense of nationalism and assertiveness in the Empire. Battles such as Gallipoli for Australia and New Zealand, and Vimy Ridge for Canada, led to increased national pride and a reluctance to remain subordinate to Britain. The dominions of Australia, New Zealand, Canada and South Africa were recognised as independent sovereign nations – and in 1939 they were granted full independence. Elsewhere, it was a different story. A number of demonstrations against British rule took place in India, for example. Troops opened fire on a Punjabi crowd peacefully gathered at the holy shrine of Amritsar in April 1919; officially, 379 men, women and children were killed and a further 1,200 injured. For many Indians, the massacre at Amritsar marked a watershed in their patience with British rule. Mahatma Gandhi spearheaded a campaign of mass civil disobedience – and, really, it was only a matter of time before the Empire was dismantled entirely.

Back home, some of the immediate ancestors of modern Britons reacted against the horror of war by indulging in unadulterated hedonism. In short, they partied. Jazz swept the land, skirts got shorter and women smoked in public. There was a fair amount of drug-taking, quite a lot of champagne-swilling and no doubt other goings-on too. The 1920s and 30s was also the period when radio came of age – 'wireless' sets appeared in most people's houses, bringing global events and organised entertainment into living rooms for the very first time. Hollywood began to dominate the fledgling pre-war cinema, introducing a new brand of popular hero, the movie star, and showing weary workers a wondrous world from across the Atlantic, beyond the grime of everyday living in Britain. Consumerism was on the increase: car ownership became more common and some of today's high street brands, like Sainsbury's and Marks & Spencer, both established in the previous century, grew. Shoppers enjoyed the treat of popping into a Joey Lyons tea shop. It was also a time of massive, mostly suburban and privately financed, house building; drive into virtually any town in Britain today and you'll see the houses of the 20s and 30s with their bow windows and mock-Tudor facades – often clustered along the main routes that, almost a century ago, were town outskirts where land was cheap.

Most people couldn't afford the luxury of enjoying themselves overmuch, though. Returning soldiers, expecting the 'land fit for heroes' promised by Prime Minister Lloyd George, were disappointed; Britain was still a land where people went hungry. The country began its recovery from the war in the context of lost overseas markets and in the face of growing competition, particularly from the USA and Japan. The return to the gold standard made British exports more expensive and employers felt that cutting wages was one solution to stay in business. Some wages – in the coal industry, for example – were already appallingly low. Mine owners faced falling productivity as well as competition from cheap German coal and pressed for longer hours with less pay. This led to the General Strike of 1926, when three million workers withdrew their labour in support of the miners. It lasted nine days and caused surprisingly little disruption; but the miners stayed on strike until poverty forced them back to work. The Great Depression, or 'Slump', of 1930 caused further misery for many thousands. Two hundred, mainly unemployed shipbuilders, marched from Jarrow to Westminster in October 1936, protesting about poverty and unemployment in the north east; the Jarrow March changed nothing (they were given their train fares home). These events became part of the folklore of industrial relations, and were remembered with bitterness well into the 1980s.

And then there was The Abdication – important enough at the time to qualify as a proper noun, though largely forgotten now. The highly respected George V died in 1936. The new king, Edward VIII, had been an extremely popular Prince of Wales. However, his affair with married American divorcee Wallis Simpson and desire to marry her provoked a potential constitutional crisis, since the Church of England disapproved of remarriage after divorce and the Monarch was head of the Church. Many also doubted whether a twice-divorced American would be unquestioningly welcomed as queen by the public – strange isn't it? Anyway, we'll never know because in the face of pressure from Prime Minister Stanley Baldwin, Edward decided to renounce the throne – the first monarch to voluntarily resign from the job – and Britain got a new king, the third in 1936, George VI. Edward married his Wallis, they were granted the title of Duke and Duchess of Windsor, invented a tie knot and maybe they lived happily ever after. History has shown this episode to be ultimately a Good Thing for Britain: Edward's judgement was questionable in some respects and he probably held Nazi sympathies. His brother, Bertie (George VI), was a wise and popular king - as well as being father of the internationally respected and much-loved Queen Elizabeth II, Britain's longest reigning monarch.

But at the end of the two decades in which nothing happened, the unthinkable did: on 3 September 1939, Britain found itself once again at war with Germany.

Could Britain have avoided war in 1939?

The failure of appeasement

Adolf Hitler's Nazi party came to power in Germany in 1933 on a programme of public works, employment and restoring both national and personal pride. This included the systematic dismemberment of the 'shameful' Treaty of Versailles, which restricted Germany's armed forces and her territory in Europe. Despite the bullying tactics of the Nazi Party's paramilitary yobos, the *Sturmabteilung* (the SA, precursors to the much more powerful and infinitely more sinister *Schutzstaffel*, the SS), many in Germany at first ignored or disbelieved the more extreme, unpleasant and outrageous aspects of Hitler's aims – though these were pretty clearly set out in his 1920s best-seller, *Mein Kampf* ('My Struggle'). The British and French governments were primarily interested in avoiding another general European conflict. Largely in defiance of the Treaty of Versailles, Hitler had increased the size of the German army, introduced military conscription, re-occupied the de-militarised Rhineland, concluded alliances with Italy and Japan and unified Germany with the land of his birth, Austria.

On 30 September 1938, the British Prime Minister, Neville Chamberlain, returned from discussions in Munich with Adolf Hitler, the Italian dictator Benito Mussolini and the French premier Edouard Daladier, over Germany's desire to annex the Sudetenland, a portion of Czechoslovakia where much of the population was ethnic German. The Czechs were not invited to the meeting, which in simple terms agreed to Germany's demands. Landing at Heston Aerodrome, Chamberlain spoke to a cheering crowd:

"The settlement of the Czechoslovakian problem, which has now

been achieved is, in my view, only the prelude to a larger settlement in which all Europe may find peace. This morning I had another talk with the German Chancellor, Herr Hitler, and here is the paper which bears his name upon it as well as mine."

Somehow, Chamberlain had persuaded Hitler to countersign what amounted to a general declaration of mutual peace and goodwill which highlighted the "desire of our two peoples never to go to war with one another again." The Prime Minister went on to see the King at Buckingham Palace, where another jubilant crowd greeted him. Back at 10 Downing Street later, he announced to those gathered outside that he had returned from Germany bringing "peace with honour". He continued: "I believe it is peace for our time." And then he told everyone to "Go home and get a nice quiet sleep."

History finds it easy to mock the apparently naive attempts of the British Prime Minister, Neville Chamberlain, to appease Chancellor Hitler. Chamberlain was a decent, civilised, man, used to dealing with like-minded people. Appeasers were in the majority in Britain, and elsewhere. With the benefit of hindsight, it is perhaps easy to accept that some, notably Winston Churchill, knew better; that Germany was rearming at an alarming rate, that Hitler was a bully and the only way to deal with bullies is to stand up to them. We know Churchill was right – but it's not that simple. A further factor is that, however inconvenient it may be to hear, at first there was a degree of sympathy for some of Hitler's policies – many people even admired them. And anyway, people said, weren't the restrictions imposed on Germany after the Great War unfair? If Germany and Austria wanted to merge into one country, wasn't that reasonable and in keeping with the principles of self-determination? It is an extreme step to interfere in the affairs of another country. Knowledge of the darker aspects of the Nazi regime was limited, and no normal person who had not experienced the brutal terror that was about to be unleashed on Europe could possibly imagine it. But a further critical factor was the memory of the First World War: the desire to avoid the slaughter being repeated and the consequent support for peace – whatever it cost – was widespread. Some believed that if this meant that Czechoslovakia lost a bit of land to Germany where the population was mostly German anyway (ignoring the fact that a good chunk of Czech industry went with it too, including the Skoda armaments works), did it really matter (unless you were Czech)? A very wise man who was in his 20s at the time (my father) once told me that his generation were the real peace generation, because they didn't just talk about it. He went on to observe how quickly attitudes change once self-interest is more obviously threatened and the metaphorical bugles call. There is a case to be made, too, for the argument that appeasement bought Britain time to re-arm and prepare.

In any event, by the time of the Munich Agreement in 1938, a good many people (including members of my own family) realised that Hitler was not a Good Thing for world peace, needed to be stopped and that war was probably inevitable. On 15 March 1939, German troops marched into the rest of Czechoslovakia. On the 1 September, Germany invaded Poland.

Britain and the Second World War 1939-45

Britain's role in the worst conflict the world has known, so far

The Second World War was the most violent and globally shattering event in history. When it finally ended, at least 60 million people lay dead; some estimates put the figure as high as 79 million. It is part of the tragedy of the war that we'll never know the true number that perished: figures for Chinese deaths, for example, range from 10 to 20 million; the Soviet Union lost 23-25 million. The sheer scale of the conflict is hard to comprehend. It was a truly worldwide struggle, with fighting taking place in the jungles of the Far East, on exotic Pacific islands, in the dusty deserts of North Africa, across vast plains or in appalling conditions of sub-zero temperatures in Russia and Eastern Europe, on pretty beaches, through tranquil farmland and in the streets of proud and ancient European towns and villages. War was waged above and below the world's oceans, from the skies, in the clouds, as well as on land. Also, as we know, the conflict did not just involve armed servicemen and women; millions of civilians were participants and victims too. Some suffered unimaginable cruelty, horror and hardship; millions of them perished; millions were displaced from their homes. Once it was all over, and most of Europe and large areas of Asia lay devastated, the balance of world power had well and truly shifted from old Europe to the new superpowers, the United States of America and the Soviet Union.

The full tragic, complex and fascinating story of the Second World War cannot be told here. Its roots lay partly in the settlements reached at the end of the First World War and in the regrettable fact that no one saw fit to put a bullet in Hitler before 1939. The war directly involved most of the world's nations to one extent or another. The principle aggressors were Germany, Japan and, until 1943, Italy – collectively referred to as the Axis powers. At the height of their supremacy, the Axis powers controlled, almost entirely through astonishing military conquest, most of Europe, South East Asia and the Pacific Islands. A particular hallmark of the conflict was the brutal nature of the totalitarian regimes of Germany, Japan and the Soviet Union, which resulted in the deliberate mistreatment and murder of civilians and prisoners of war. This included, in the case of Nazi Germany, policies that not only discriminated against individuals who did not conform to a twisted notion of racial purity, but also sponsored the slaughter of many – not least approximately 6 million Jews – in work and death camps. The conclusion of the war was the defeat of Germany and Japan by an alliance led by the United Kingdom, the United States of America and the Soviet Union.

Physically, Britain suffered relatively lightly compared with other countries. Its villages and towns were not devastated to the same extent as those of, say, Poland, France, Germany and the Soviet Union; it did not have to endure the terror of occupation (apart from the Channel Islands). Even so, the war was a shocking event for Britain; 450,900 of its people died, 67,100 of which were civilians who mostly perished in the destruction of large parts of British cities by aerial bombardment. And at the end of it, as well as being a greatly diminished power, Britain was broke.

For most people in Britain, their experience of being at war again began with the measured tones of Prime Minister Neville Chamberlain coming from the radio on 3 September 1939:

"I am speaking to you from the Cabinet Room at 10 Downing Street. This morning the British Ambassador in Berlin handed the German Government a final note stating

that, unless we hear from them by 11 o'clock that they were prepared at once to withdraw their troops from Poland, a state of war would exist between us. I have to tell you now that no such undertaking has been received, and that consequently this country is at war with Germany."

Then the air raid sirens sounded, disrupting Sunday lunch. Britain and her ally, France, were in fact physically powerless to assist Poland and, after a brief campaign and a surprise invasion by the Soviet Union from the east (in accordance with the secret Nazi-Soviet Pact signed just the previous week), independent Poland ceased to exist for the next 50 years. British forces dispatched to France twiddled their thumbs and played football during a period nicknamed 'the phoney war', while, at home, people coped with the blackout (which resulted in thousands of deaths on the road before bombing even started) and evacuated their children from cities in anticipation of devastating air raids. Government propaganda and control was persuasive and highly effective. The 'Dig for Victory' campaign eventually saw parks and gardens turned over to growing vegetables. In January 1940, rationing was introduced.

April 1940: in a disastrous campaign to deny Germany access to Swedish iron ore and control of Norway, British and French troops were routed by the Germans – who had also occupied strategically-placed Denmark in just 6 hours while they were about it. The German Blitzkrieg (lightning war) went on to sweep through the Netherlands, Belgium and France, starting on 10 May. Holland surrendered on 14 May, Belgium on 28. Between 26 May and 4 June, Britain evacuated 198,000 of its forces and 140,000 French, from Dunkirk – thus creating a story that has become part of British folklore, not least the part played by hundreds of small privately-owned boats that crossed the Channel to help. It takes particular genius to portray defeat in such a positive way, but there is no denying the achievement. (It is perhaps a good moment to mention that the story of Britain's military war is told in hundreds of movies, most of which seem to star John Mills, Richard Attenborough or Michael Redgrave - look them up if you don't know). Some in France regarded Britain's decision to evacuate forces from Dunkirk as a betrayal. Almost 192,000 additional Allied personnel were evacuated from other ports in France in late June. Most of the British Expeditionary Force's equipment – tanks, trucks and so forth – was left in France. On 22 June, France surrendered.

After the fall of France, Britain was on its own. It was in no position to beat Germany at the time, but could do enough to ensure that Germany would not win. The leadership of its new Prime Minister, Winston Churchill, was inspirational, and decisive. Many voices in Britain called for a negotiated peace; Churchill recognised the long-term folly of this course of action and galvanised resistance. He later wrote, "I felt...that all my past life had been but a preparation for this hour and for this trial". His strategic vision was masterful, his work-rate phenomenal; in his speeches, as journalist Ed Murrow noted, "He took the English language and sent it into battle."

"We shall go on to the end. We shall fight in France, we shall fight on the seas and oceans, we shall fight with growing confidence and growing strength in the air, we shall defend our island, whatever the cost may be. We shall fight on the beaches, we shall fight on the landing grounds, we shall fight in the fields and in the streets, we shall fight in the hills; we shall never surrender, and if, which I do not for a moment believe, this island or a large part of it were subjugated and starving, then our Empire beyond the seas, armed and guarded by the British Fleet, would carry on the struggle, until, in God's good time, the New World, with all its power and might, steps forth to the rescue and the liberation of the old." - Churchill – House of Commons, 4 June 1940.

As a prelude to invasion, the German Luftwaffe needed to achieve superiority over the Royal Air Force. What became known as the Battle of Britain was fought mainly in the skies over southern England during the summer and early autumn of 1940. However, the Luftwaffe consistently underestimated the numbers of aircraft the RAF had, misunderstood RAF command and control capabilities (including RADAR), which were the best in the world, and made a fatal tactical error in switching attacks from military to civilian targets. Despite initial inferiority in numbers, the RAF had the advantages of fighting over its own territory – fuel limitations meant that German aircraft had a restricted amount of time over Britain and any trained aircrew that were shot down were either killed or taken prisoner, whereas surviving RAF pilots could be returned to battle. Further, with two classic fighter aircraft, the Spitfire and the Hurricane, they enjoyed at least technical equality with the Germans. Finally, the skill and bravery of RAF fighter pilots ('the Few') helped ensure that the Germans failed to achieve air superiority; the invasion was postponed indefinitely and the Battle of Britain was won. Incidentally, 20% of RAF Battle of Britain pilots came from overseas, including from Poland, Czechoslovakia, France, New Zealand, Australia and Canada – as well as from neutral Ireland and the USA.

Notwithstanding the postponed invasion, from September 1940 – May 1941, Germany launched what became known as 'the Blitz' – a bombing campaign against Britain intended to cripple industrial production and destroy civilian morale. Most heavily targeted was London, which endured 57 consecutive night attacks, but other major cities were hit too including Liverpool, Birmingham, Plymouth, Bristol, Glasgow, Southampton, Portsmouth, Coventry, Hull, Manchester, Belfast, Sheffield, Newcastle, Nottingham and Cardiff. Air raids dropped off when

Germany's attention switched to the invasion of the Soviet Union in June 1941. But civilian deaths increased again in 1944 with the arrival of V1 'Doodlebugs' (pilotless flying bombs), followed by V2 rockets - which the British government initially passed off as gas explosions, for fear of widespread panic.

The Blitz failed to achieve its objectives. Despite that, the RAF set about doing the same thing to Germany. Once the US Air Force was engaged from mid-1942, the Americans operated by day whilst the RAF worked at night. The allied bombing campaign is still controversial. More than 300,000 German civilians were killed, including during massive raids on Hamburg and Dresden where the concentration of high explosive was so intense that it produced fire storms. Thousands of citizens of occupied countries died too, as well as prisoners of war. 55,000 young men of RAF bomber command perished – the highest casualty-rate for any British unit in the war. But the air attacks did gradually erode Nazi industrial capacity and also tied up resources that would otherwise have been used against the Soviet Union. By the time the Allies invaded Europe in 1944, they enjoyed complete air superiority and had disrupted German transportation, which included vital oil supplies.

In the Atlantic and Mediterranean, ships carrying food, armaments, oil and other essentials were sunk at an alarming rate by German submarines – 'U-boats' (an abbreviation of *Unterseeboot*) – many of these operating from bases in occupied France. Dependent on supplies from Canada and the USA, winning the Battle of the Atlantic was vital for Britain's survival. Gradually, better organisation of convoys, improved intelligence, anti-submarine techniques and air cover began to reverse the trend. But the ships also had to battle against the sea, which could be as cruel an enemy as anything man-made. On the Arctic Convoys dispatched to get vital aid to the Soviet Union, there was the added peril of sub-zero temperatures, where sea-spray turned to ice on men's faces, the weight of ice on decks threatened to take ships under and a man overboard would only survive minutes before freezing to death.

Following Italy's declaration of war on 10 June 1940, British forces in Egypt undertook a series of successful raids against Italian troops in Libya. The Italians invaded Egypt in September 1940 and the resulting counter-attack prompted Hitler to send reinforcements to come to his beleaguered ally's aid. The arrival of the German Africa Korps under the command of the talented *Generalleutnant* Erwin Rommel completely changed the dynamics of war in North Africa and, at one point, there was concern that Cairo might fall. The Germans were also triumphant in Greece, Crete and Yugoslavia. The Battle of Alamein from October 1942 marked a turn of the tide; British, Australian, New Zealand, South African and Indian troops under Lieutenant-General Bernard Montgomery pushed the German and Italian forces back. Churchill commented, "This is not the end. It is not even the beginning of the end. But it is, perhaps, the end of the beginning."

In fact, 1941 was a defining year. In June, Hitler launched his long-intended attack on the Soviet Union. In December, the United States entered the war following Japan's infamous surprise attack on Pearl Harbor. Bizarrely, Hitler declared war on the USA and, significantly, President Roosevelt agreed a policy of 'Germany first' with Churchill. From that point, the outcome of the war was not in doubt – it was a matter of how long, and at what cost. The huge material resources of the United States and the enormous manpower (and casualties) expended by the Soviet Union were probably the two most decisive factors in achieving ultimate victory. A further factor was British intelligence. Project Ultra, based at Bletchley Park, used pioneering technology to break German codes; it has been estimated this shortened the war by two years.

The Japanese, who had been waging an aggressive war against China since 1931, bombed British Hong Kong at the same time as attacking Pearl Harbor. They conducted a swift campaign in South East Asia and the Pacific which was a disaster for the British. Malaya was taken in January 1942, and when Singapore fell in February with more than 80,000 British, Australian and Indian troops being taken prisoner it was the greatest capitulation in British military history. Eventually, Japanese forces threatened India. The war in South East Asia and the Pacific was a bitter one against a relentless foe that believed it was shameful to surrender, and who often fought to the last man. The Americans slogged to retake island after island from the Japanese, whilst British, Australian and Indian forces sought to gain the upper hand in Burma and Borneo. Allied prisoners of the Japanese, as well as civilians in territories occupied by them, suffered cruel treatment from a foe who displayed a warped medieval disregard for humanity.

An epic struggle took place in Eastern Europe, where the war between the Soviet Union and Nazi Germany was fought on a scale and with levels of barbarism that are hard to understand. Initial German success was followed by the onset of the Russian winter and its people's amazing capacity for resistance under their dictator, Joseph Stalin.

The Russians began counter-attacking in 1942, by 1943 were pushing the Germans back and by August 1944 they had re-taken Poland. The British and Americans invaded North West Africa in 1942 and Italy in 1943. Britain in early 1944 was an armed fortress in preparation for the invasion of Western Europe. This meticulously planned 'Operation Overlord' was launched from southern ports in Devon, Dorset, Hampshire and Sussex and, on 6 June (D-Day), British, Canadian and American troops landed on five beaches in Normandy, code-named Utah, Omaha (American), Gold, Sword (British) and Juno (Canadian). After tough fighting against what many experts believe was the most effective army ever, and a few arguably self-inflicted set-backs, superior resources prevailed. France and Belgium were liberated and by March 1945, Allied forces were in Germany itself. In April, US and Soviet troops met on the Elbe. With Russian troops in Berlin, Hitler committed suicide on 30 April and on 8 May Germany surrendered unconditionally.

The end in the east came suddenly. British and allied forces took Mandalay in March 1945 and Rangoon in May. The stage was set for the invasion of Japan. But on 6 August the US dropped an atomic bomb ('Little Boy') on Hiroshima. On 8 August, the Soviet Union declared war on Japan and 1 million Soviet soldiers invaded Japanese-occupied Manchuria. A second atomic bomb ('Fat Man') was dropped on Nagasaki on 9 August and, on 14 August, Japan too surrendered unconditionally. The war was over.

Britain after 1945

The recent background to our consumer society

The Britons that dusted themselves down and emerged on the winning side in 1945 were delirious with joy and relief that it was all over. There was a terrible human price to pay, of course. And if the Britain of those days seems a little drab to our more modern eyes, it's not just because most of the movies were in monochrome; times were really tough. There wasn't a lot of cash, the country had virtually bankrupted itself fighting the war, cities needed rebuilding, homelessness was an acute problem and there was still rationing - which continued until 1954.

The story of Britain since 1945 could be described as one of profound change and often painful adjustment. Our very recent ancestors would probably gaze in wonder at the place they have helped to create. It isn't all their work, of course; external influences have played their part too. However, whatever its detractors may say, Britain is more democratic now than it has ever been and class distinctions are more blurred. It is a cleaner, materially wealthier, nation. Its people live longer, are generally better fed (if not necessarily healthier), better clothed (possibly), better educated (allegedly), and with new ambitions – some even aspire to appearing on reality TV shows. It's a more crowded place now. From 1951 to 2011, the population of the United Kingdom grew from around 50 million to about 63 million, mostly as a consequence of immigration. Immigration, particularly from the old colonies (largely a result of the British Nationality Act of 1948), has helped transform society, including eating habits and religion. In 1945, you might have tucked into a meal of pork faggots with mashed potato, or a nice liver casserole; these days, you are more likely to eat a stir-fry or chicken tikka masala. In 1945 most people were, at least nominally, Christian in their beliefs; in 2011, 59% of England and Wales admitted to being Christian, 25% confessed to having no religious beliefs whatsoever and the next biggest group, at 5%, claimed to be Muslim. Even language has changed; regional differences are definitely still there, but (sadly in my view), they're less distinct. Overseas influences have crept into everyday speech, from the United States, Australia and the West Indies. Moral codes have changed – it was unusual, and frowned upon, for unmarried couples to 'live in sin' in 1945, there was more censorship and homosexuality and abortion were both illegal. There's a greater emphasis on youth in modern Britain ("Quick, hire someone under thirty while they still know everything."). Industry, the power house of empire – mining, textiles, engineering, shipbuilding, manufacturing – has declined such that the old industrial areas of South Wales, lowland Scotland, the north and midlands of England, with their big sooty towns and buildings, would be virtually unrecognisable to their mid-20th century citizens. Some places have been reincarnated as something else, others appear to be deceased; some are museums. Most people work in the service sector now. According to the Office for National Statistics, "by 2011 around 80% of workers were in the service industry and around 10% in manufacturing."

Traditional seaside towns are a shadow of their former selves, often a little tacky and frayed round the edges, but exude a kind of proud nostalgic charm. The motorway network grew from the 1960s, car ownership has rocketed, the railway network is much smaller – but it's a more mobile lifestyle. Travelling more than ten miles to work doesn't raise an eyebrow in the 21st century, and when children reach adulthood they are less likely to stay in the same town as their parents. Britain, so long isolating itself from Europe, eventually joined the European Community – and then narrowly voted to leave it. We even have decimal coinage these days – though you still buy beer in pints, thank God. Wind farms have appeared on horizons, on land and shoreline. Wales, Scotland and Northern Ireland each has a form of devolved government. Sooner or later, England will probably need a similar arrangement. The pace of change since the 1980s has been particularly astonishing – largely driven by the micro-chip, of course, without which you wouldn't be looking at this, dear reader.

It could be argued that progress, youth and consumerism are the new religions. In 1945, people were certainly looking forward, not backwards. Many felt they had to have been fighting for something rather more than to simply beat the bad guys and survive. Churchill had succeeded majestically in leading Britain to victory, but failed to sell a vision for the future; under his brand of Conservatism, life would just be more of the same. However, the Labour party promised a New Jerusalem – and won the 1945 general election by a landslide, with 393 MPs. Few expected Churchill to lose; it was shattering for the Great Old Man, and a political earthquake. Prime Minister Clement Atlee's Labour government shaped Britain more than any other until Margaret Thatcher's Conservative one 35 years later. Based on the far-reaching proposals of the liberal Beveridge Report of 1942, Labour committed itself to a cradle to grave welfare state, funded by taxation, created the National Health Service and nationalised basic industries. But, simultaneously, the new government had to cope with empty coffers, an ailing Empire and a whole new international situation. Modern critics of austerity economics should look into history to see how the state tried to deliver utopian socialism in the straitened circumstances of the late 1940s and early 1950s. The lack of cash was helped by a loan from the USA – Britain was already massively in debt to the USA for materials provided during the war – followed by huge assistance under the so-called Marshall Plan to help regenerate Europe as a whole. The loan was finally repaid in 2006.

Recovery, and Labour's radical programme, was almost scuppered by the weather. The winter of 1947, one of the worst on record, took Britain to the brink of starvation as coal shortages ground transport and production to a halt.

There was an inability – or reluctance – to comprehend and accept Britain's new place in the world. In 1945, Britain still controlled about a quarter of the world's population. But it could no longer afford to be the power it had been, though an enormous amount of public money has been spent trying to be. It is understandable, even if it makes no sense in hindsight. Some argue that high levels of defence spending, perhaps encouraged by its alleged 'special relationship' with the USA, has helped deliver less economic prosperity for Britain than might otherwise have been the case. Arguably, the money could have been put to better use – for example by investing more in education and in Britain's already ailing industries. By and large, successive governments – Conservative and Labour - carried on the basic principles set by Atlee's 1945 government until, by the 1970s, it had become clear that something had gone badly wrong; Britain seemed to be in economic and political crisis, with undemocratic trades unions frequently at odds with the elected government. The story of Britain since 1945 is also partly one of successive governments' ability to balance, not always successfully, limited resources.

The Empire has gone; inappropriate now, it could not survive in a new post-war order, particularly after its subject peoples had seen that the old European imperial powers in the Far East could be beaten by an Asiatic one, the Japanese. India, 'the Jewel in the Crown', was the first to go, in 1947. It was not a happy transfer of power; the partition into Muslim Pakistan and everyone else in India witnessed hideous and tragic loss of life. One by one, through the 1950s right up to the 1980s, colonies gained independence. It was often a painful, violent, process; and occasionally embarrassing. The last territory to go (so far) was Hong Kong, handed back to China in 1997. But if Britain needed a reminder of its changed circumstances, it came as early as 1956 when, in ill-conceived collusion with Israel and France, British and French troops invaded Egypt as a reaction to Egyptian President Nasser's nationalisation of the Suez Canal. Following the angry threat of economic sanctions from its close ally, the United States, Britain was forced into a humiliating withdrawal and the Prime Minister, Anthony Eden, resigned. Washington, not London, now called the shots. Yet Britain still somehow manages to be a global player - kind of – and is a permanent member of the UN Security Council. The Royal Navy no longer rules the waves, but British forces have been deployed somewhere almost every day since 1945 and, according to the Royal British Legion, more than 12,000 servicemen and women have died or have been seriously injured on active service from that year to the present.

So we need to briefly mention the Cold War, because this informed so much of today's Britain. The victorious allies in the Second World War had one common aim – the defeat of Hitler's Germany: but beyond that, each had a different vision of the future based on their respective histories and diametrically opposed ideologies. Everyone wanted security – no one more so than the Soviet Union's odious dictator, Stalin, who was understandably anxious to protect his country from further invasion. Stalin harboured a deep mistrust of the west. Both the Soviet Union and the United States mistrusted Britain, because of its imperial position, but Britain lacked the muscle of its two allies. So there they all were, with huge armies in Europe – and the US with the atom bomb. Somehow, everyone agreed in the creation of the United Nations – an effort to do rather better than its predecessor, the League of Nations. But in 1946, that old statesman Churchill summed up what many in the west already thought, in a speech in Fulton, Missouri, when he said, "From Stettin in the Baltic to Trieste in the Adriatic, an iron curtain has descended across the continent." It was recognition of the seemingly insurmountable differences between totalitarian communism and western capitalist democracy. In 1947, President Truman announced the 'Truman Doctrine', which essentially pledged US support for "free people who are resisting attempted subjugation by armed minorities or by outside pressures" – and the fight against communism drove much US foreign policy until the Reagan era of the 1980s. By 1949 NATO, the North Atlantic Treaty Organisation, had been formed – principally as a defensive alliance against aggression by the Soviet Union, and in reaction to the perceived threat. The United Kingdom was a founder member of both the UN and NATO. Essentially, the Cold War escalated in wars fought directly or indirectly by the US and her allies against Soviet-backed forces in other countries – especially ex-colonial territories such as Korea and Vietnam. By the early '50s, the Soviet Union had a viable atomic bomb and in 1955 it founded the Warsaw Pact, as a counter-organisation to NATO. Britain, having helped the US develop the bomb in the first place, made its own in 1952. And so it went on. Those who grew up in Britain from the 1950s-80s half expected a nuclear holocaust at any time. Eventually, both sides arrived at the doctrine of Mutually Assured Destruction, or MAD (yes, really), which essentially says that because each side has the capacity to wipe each other out, no one will make the first strike. So that's alright then.

Now, as many writers have pointed out, like it or not, we are all children of Margaret Thatcher. Thatcher was Britain's first woman Prime Minister, held that office from 1979-1990, transformed the country and continues to divide opinion. She controversially introduced 'the right to buy' for tenants of local authority homes and embarked on a radical programme of privatisation of nationalised industries, including the utilities (energy and water suppliers), market deregulation, reform of trade unions and lower direct taxation. As with the great reforming Labour government of 1945, successive administrations have stuck with many of the changes Thatcher brought about. Yet she would not recognise much of the Britain she helped to shape – and watching newsreels of the 1970s and '80s is to peek into another world. And so Britain has morphed from whatever it used to be to whatever you think it is now. Like anywhere else, it's not perfect and it is, to re-use the cliché, a product of its past. But its past is a fascinating one and has made it a unique, and somewhat special, place. For all its faults, I'm rather fond of it.

I wonder what will happen next?

TO BE CONTINUED

TIMELINES

I PREHISTORIC TIMELINE

c700-800,000BC
The earliest humanoid presence in Britain at Happisburgh.

c485,000BC
Boxgrove Man (*Homo Heidelbergensis*) – the oldest humanoid fossil found in Britain so far.

c350,000BC
Swanscombe woman.

c25,000BC
Arrival of *Homo Sapiens* - our early ancestors.

c12-10,000BC
Permanent human settlement begins.

c8,000-6,000BC
Last Ice Age ends in Europe.

c6,000BC
Last land bridge separating Britain from the rest of Europe was swept away.

c4,000-2,500BC
Neolithic period - the first farmers, possibly arrivals from the east.
Early enclosures and burial chambers.
Later Neolithic period sees the construction of henges and stone circles.

c3,000BC
Construction of Stonehenge begun.

c2,500-750BC
Bronze Age - round barrows (burial chambers), villages and the first hill forts are built. 'The Beaker People'.

c1,200BC
Construction of roundhouses.

c750BC
The Iron Age. The arrival of the Celts, probably in waves. Hill forts are a typical feature of settlement.

c500BC
Construction of brochs in Scotland.

c300BC
Somerset lake villages.

c100BC
Coins are in use.

55BC
Immediately before the Roman invasion, Britain is peopled by a number of different tribes. Their names come to us from Roman writers and include the *Durotriges* in modern Dorset/Wiltshire, the *Atrebates* in parts of Sussex, Hampshire and Berkshire, the *Iceni* in Norfolk and Suffolk, the *Brigantes* in Yorkshire, Durham and Lancashire, the *Votadini* in south east Scotland, the *Caledones* in the Highlands and the Picts in north east Scotland.

55 and 54BC
Julius Caesar invades southern Britain. He exacts tributes from defeated tribes but does not stay.

43AD
Full-scale Roman conquest of Britain begins.

II ROMAN TIMELINE

43AD
Full-scale Roman conquest of Britain begins, ordered by the Emperor Claudius. Troops land near present-day Richborough (*Rutupiae*), Kent.

51AD
British resistance leader Caratacus (or Caractacus) is captured.

60 or 61AD
Boudicca, Queen of the Iceni (a tribe located in present-day Norfolk), is defeated after leading a rebellion in which the Roman towns of Colchester (*Camulodunum*), St Albans (*Verulamium*) and London (*Londinium*) were burned to the ground.

71AD
The Romans campaign in the north of what is now England, reaching the area around Carlisle (*Luguvalium*) in 74AD

78AD
The Romans conquer present-day Wales and destroy the sacred Druid sites on *Mona* (Anglesey).

84AD
The Caledonian tribes are defeated at the Battle of *Mons Graupius*. The Roman armies have got as far as modern-day Aberdeenshire, Scotland - the furthest extent of their conquest - though Scotland was never settled like England and Wales.

Timelines

122AD
Construction of Hadrian's Wall, from the River Tyne in the east to the Solway firth in the west, begins.

142AD
Construction of the Antonine Wall, from the Firth of Forth in the east to the Clyde in the west, begins.

163AD
The Antonine Wall is abandoned.

c200-300AD
Christianity arrives in Britain.

211AD
Britain is divided into two provinces, *Britannia Superior* (Upper Britain) with its capital in London and *Britannia Inferior* (Lower Britain) with its capital in York (*Eboracum*).

c260AD
The Romans start to build coastal defences to discourage attacks from Germanic raiders. The defences come to be known as 'the Saxon Shore', a military command stretching from Norfolk to Hampshire in modern Britain.

306AD
Constantine is declared Emperor by the army in Britain.

313AD
The Edict of Milan grants toleration of Christianity.

367AD
Near simultaneous raids on Britain by Picts from Scotland, Scots from Ireland and Franks and Anglo-Saxons from Germany. Coastal defences are overwhelmed.

370sAD
An Asiatic tribe, the Huns, appear in Western Europe. Germanic tribes, such as the Visigoths, begin to threaten the Empire.

397AD
St Ninian, Scotland's legendary first Christian missionary, allegedly lands in Strathclyde.

400AD
Troops are withdrawn from Britain to help defend Italy against the Goths. By this time, independent kingdoms had been established in Strathclyde, Gododdin and Galloway, immediately north of Hadrian's Wall.

410AD
Attacks on Britain continue. British leaders make a vain appeal for help from the Emperor Honorius in Rome. It was in this year that Rome fell to the Goths.

410-449AD
It is generally accepted that Roman rule in Britain gradually fades away at around this time - though a Roman way of life continues for a while.

III EARLY MEDIEVAL TIMELINE

449
The traditional date, according to the monk Bede, for the arrival of Anglo-Saxons in South-East England.

c500
Saxons are settled in southern England.

516
A possible date for the mysterious Battle of Mount Badon, in which the Britons under an unknown leader defeat the Saxons. The battle later became associated with the legendary King Arthur - the last of 12 fabled battles he is said to have fought.

c550-c650
Angles, Saxons and Jutes conquer lowland England. They evolve multiple 'kingdoms'. British culture is generally extinguished from England but continues in western Britain.

563
St Columba founds a monastery on the island of Iona.

596
Pope Gregory saw Angles in Rome's slave market and dispatches Augustine to convert them to Christianity.

597
St Augustine lands in Thanet to convert the pagan Saxons in Kent.

602

King Ethelbert of Kent donates a site in Canterbury for a new cathedral. His Frankish wife, Bertha, was already Christian.

627

Edwin of Northumbria is the first Christian king in the north of England.

629

In the wider context - Muhammad seizes Mecca.

635

St Aidan founds a monastery at Lindisfarne

c650

By the end of the 7th century, there are 7 main Anglo-Saxon Kingdoms in what is now modern England: Northumbria, Mercia, East Anglia, Wessex, Kent, Sussex and Essex. To the south-west are the West Welsh in *Dumnonia* (Devon) and *Kernow* (Cornwall). Further British kingdoms are Powys, Gwynedd, Gwent, *Rheged* (Cumbria) and Strathclyde.

654

St Cedd, a Northumbrian priest in the Celtic tradition, set out to evangelise the heathen East Saxons.

664

Synod of Whitby - determined that the English church would follow Rome, rather than the Celtic, Christian tradition.

685

Battle of Dunnichen (or *Dun Nechtain*) - King Bridei's Picts stop the northern expansion of the Northumbrian Angles.

731

Bede completes his 'History of the English Church and People'.

757

Offa becomes King of Mercia. He orders the construction of a defensive earthwork between Mercia and Powys, now known as Offa's Dyke.

789

Vikings raid Dorset - the first recorded Viking attack on Britain.

793

Vikings attack Lindisfarne.

795

Vikings attack Iona.

829

Egbert, King of Wessex, conquers Mercia.

843

Kenneth MacAlpin united Picts and Scots to form one kingdom.

867

The Danes capture York.

869

Edmund, King of East Anglia, is martyred by the Danes.

870
Vikings destroy Dumbarton, stronghold of the Kingdom of Strathclyde.

871-900
The reign of Alfred the Great, King of Wessex.

877
Danes attack Chippenham at Christmas, forcing Alfred into hiding in Athelney, Somerset.

878
Alfred defeats the Danes at Edington (*Ethandun*), Wiltshire.

886
Alfred makes a treaty with the Danes that secures the Kingdoms of Wessex and Mercia and establishes the area of 'Danelaw' north of the Thames and south of the Tees.

925
Athelstan is crowned King of Wessex. He is generally accepted as the first king of all England.

927
Having defeated the Danes in the north, Athelstan accepts the submission of the kings of the Scots, Strathclyde Welsh, Cumbria and the Earl of Northumbria at Eamont Bridge, Cumbria.

937
A combined invasion of Vikings, Welsh and Scots is crushed by Athelstan at Brunanburh (no one knows where this was).

978
Edward, King of England, is martyred at Corfe, Dorset.

991
Battle of Maldon - an English army is defeated by invading Vikings in Essex. The King, Ethelred, pays Danegeld (ie protection money) to buy peace.

1002
St Brice's Day massacre - King Ethelred orders the massacre of all Danes in England.

1013
Swein Forkbeard invades England. Once again, the Danes rule.

1016
Cnut of Denmark becomes King of England.

1017
Cnut marries Emma of Normandy, the widow of Ethelred. Cnut divided England into four earldoms - Northumbria Wessex, Mercia and East Anglia - each at one time kingdoms in their own right.

1018
Battle of Carham – date and details uncertain. Malcolm II, King of Alba, defeated Uhtred of Northumbria, becomes first king of a united Scotland and establishes a border very similar to today's.

1040
Macbeth defeats Duncan and becomes King of Scotland.

1042

Edward the Confessor becomes King of England.

1066

Edward the Confessor dies. Harold becomes King of England. England is invaded by Vikings from the north, culminating in the Battle of Stamford Bridge, and Normans from the south leading to the defeat of Harold at the Battle of Hastings. William, Duke of Normandy, is crowned King of England on 25 December.

IV LATER MEDIEVAL TIMELINE

1066
The Norman Conquest. William the Conqueror is crowned King of England on Christmas Day.

1069
The 'harrying of the North' - William I viciously puts down rebellion in the north of England.

1072
The Treaty of Abernethy. King Malcolm III of Scotland acknowledges King William I of England as his feudal overlord.

1086
The Domesday Survey of England – a unique record of who owned what.

1091
Malcolm III of Scotland invades England. He is beaten back by William II (Rufus) and in the process loses land which is now part of the English county of Cumbria.

1096
Probable date for the foundation of Oxford University.

1114
Henry I of England invades Wales.

1139-53
The 'Anarchy' - civil war in England between followers of Stephen and Matilda, both claimants to the crown of England.

1154
Henry II becomes King of England. His so-called Angevin Empire included England, Normandy, Maine, Brittany, Anjou, Touraine, Aquitaine, Gascony and Toulouse.

1169
English conquest of Ireland begins.

1170
The murder of Thomas a Becket in Canterbury Cathedral.

1190
Richard I ('the Lionheart') and the Third Crusade.

1209
Foundation of Cambridge University.

1215
The barons rebel against King John and force him to agree to Magna Carta.

1216
The French invade England.

1217
Battle of Lincoln - French Prince Louis and his English baron allies are defeated by the young King Henry III's army under William Marshal, 1st Earl of Pembroke.

1237
Treaty of York determines the Anglo-Scottish border.

1263
Scots fight the Norwegians at the Battle of Largs. Though indecisive, Norwegian power began to decline afterwards.

1264
Battle of Lewes - Simon de Montfort captures King Henry III.

1265
Simon de Montfort summons a parliament - and is subsequently killed at the Battle of Evesham.

1267
Henry III of England acknowledges Llywelyn ap Gruffydd's lordship in Wales.

1277-82
Edward I of England invades and annexes Wales.

1290
Edward I expels Jews from England

1292
Edward I selects John Balliol as king of the Scots.

1295
Edward I summons 'the Model Parliament'. As well as barons and bishops, it included representatives from counties, boroughs and cities.

1297
Scotland's Andy Murray and William Wallace defeat an English army at Stirling Bridge.

1298
William Wallace is defeated by the English at Falkirk.

1301
Edward I declares the first English Prince of Wales –
the future Edward II.

1305
William Wallace is executed.

1306
Robert the Bruce is crowned King of Scotland.

1312
The suppression of the Knights Templar.

1314
Scots under Robert the Bruce defeat the English at the
Battle of Bannockburn.

1320
Declaration of Arbroath - Scottish declaration of
independence.

1327
The murder of Edward II in Berkeley Castle.

1337-1453
Hundred Years War between England and France.

1333
Scots lose Berwick on Tweed to the English.

1346
English under Edward III defeat French at the Battle of
Crecy.

1348
The Black Death comes to Britain.

1356
English forces under Edward, the Black Prince, defeat the French at the Battle of Poitiers.

1371
Robert II becomes the first Stuart king of Scotland.

1381
The Peasants' Revolt.

1387
Geoffrey Chaucer begins the Canterbury Tales.

1399
Richard II deposed by Henry IV and subsequently starved to death.

1413
Foundation of St Andrews University.

1415
English under Henry V defeat French at the Battle of Agincourt.

1420
Treaty of Troyes - agreement that Henry V of England and his heirs will inherit the throne of France on the death of the then King of France, Charles VI. Henry marries Charles' daughter, Catherine of Valois.

1422
Henry V dies. His 9-month old son becomes Henry VI and, on the death of his French grandfather, Charles VI, King of France too.

1440
Eton College founded by Henry VI.

1450
Jack Cade's rebellion.

1451
University of Glasgow founded.

1453
French defeat the English at the Battle of Castillon. This marks the end of the Hundred Years War. England has lost all of its extensive territories in France; only the town of Calais remains in English hands.

1454
In the wider context – in Mainz, Gutenberg publishes the Bible, the first book in Europe printed using moveable type.

1455-85
The Wars of the Roses (the Cousins' War) between the Houses of Lancaster and York.

1455
First Battle of St Albans.

1461
Battle of Towton - "the bloodiest battle in English history".

1471
Battle of Tewkesbury results in victory for the Yorkists under Edward IV. Henry VI is murdered in the Tower of London.
Scotland formally annexes the Shetland and Orkney islands.

1476
Caxton publishes the first book printed in England.

1483
Sudden death of Edward IV. His sons, Edward, heir to the throne, and younger brother Richard, disappear. Edward IV's brother, Richard, makes himself King Richard III.

1485
Battle of Bosworth. Henry Tudor defeats Richard III and starts a new dynasty as Henry VII.

V TUDOR TIMELINE

1485
Henry Tudor becomes King Henry VII of England after his victory at the Battle of Bosworth.

1487
Lambert Simnel challenges for the throne, pretending to be the son of Edward IV. The rebels are defeated at the Battle of East Stoke in Nottinghamshire and Simnel is given a job in the royal kitchens.

1492
In a wider context – Christopher Columbus arrives in the Bahamas instead of Japan.

1495
University of Aberdeen founded.

1497
Commissioned by Henry VII, John Cabot (Giovanni Caboto, a Venetian) discovers Newfoundland.

1503
James IV of Scotland marries Margaret, daughter of Henry VII of England.

1509
Henry VIII marries Katherine of Aragon and becomes king of England.

1512
England at war with France and Scotland.

1513
Scotland invades England and is defeated at the Battle of Flodden. James IV of Scotland is amongst those killed.

1517
In a wider context - in Wittenberg, Martin Luther nailed his 95 Thesis to the door of All Saints' Church, or the *Schlosskirche*, questioning excesses and corruption in the Roman Catholic Church.

1519
In a wider context – Portuguese explorer Ferdinand Magellan leads a Spanish sponsored expedition that resulted in the first circumnavigation of the globe.

1522-25
England at war with France.

1526
In Worms, Germany, John Tyndale publishes a translation of the New Testament in English.

1528
England at war with Spain.

1529
Henry VIII seizes Hampton Court from Cardinal Wolsey.

1530
Death of Cardinal Wolsey.

1533
Archbishop Thomas Cranmer annuls Henry VIII's marriage with Katherine of Aragon and Henry marries Anne Boleyn.

1534
The Act of Supremacy - Henry becomes Head of the Church of England - the official start of the English Reformation.

1535
The dissolution of monasteries in England begins. Sir Thomas More is executed.

1536
Anne Boleyn is executed. Henry VIII marries Jane Seymour.
The Pilgrimage of Grace – a rebellion, particularly in Yorkshire, against Henry VIII's religious reforms.
The first Laws in Wales Act, often incorrectly referred to as the Act of Union between England and Wales, abolished the Marcher Lords, established Welsh administrative areas and MPs and aimed to harmonise Welsh administration and law with English.

1537
Jane Seymour dies having given birth to a son, the future King Edward VI.

1539
Publication of Henry VIII's Great Bible in English.

1540
Henry VIII marries and swiftly divorces Anne of Cleves. Thomas Cromwell, principal architect of the Reformation, is executed. Henry marries Kathryn Howard, his 5th wife.

1541
Henry VIII makes himself King of Ireland.

Timelines

1542
The English defeat an invading Scottish army at Solway Moss.
Kathryn Howard is executed.

1543-51
The rough wooing - Henry's violent and failed attempt to force an alliance with Scotland by marring his son Edward to the future Mary, Queen of Scots.

1543
The second Laws in Wales Act tightened provisions of the Act of 1536.
England was at war with France.
Henry VIII married for the last time - Katherine Parr survived him.

1547
Henry VIII dies. Edward VI becomes King of England. The new king is determined to reform the English church and make it more Protestant.

1549
The First Act of Uniformity establishes the Book of Common Prayer, a standard form of worship across England and Wales.
The Kett Rebellion in Norfolk – the largest of several rebellions at the time, mostly in protest against landlords' enclosures of common land. The rebels captured Norwich, England's second city, but were eventually defeated.

1553
Edward dies. Lady Jane Grey was uncrowned 'Queen for 9 days' before Mary, the daughter of Henry VIII and Katherine of Aragon, came to the throne. Mary is determined to return England to Roman Catholicism.

1553
Protestants begin to be persecuted.

1554
Mary marries the King of Spain, Philip II.
The Wyatt Rebellion – arising from fear that England would be ruled by Spain. Lady Jane Grey is executed as a precaution.

1555
Prominent Protestant churchmen Hugh Latimer and Nicholas Ridley are burned at the stake.

1556
Former Archbishop Cranmer is burned at the stake.

1557
War with France.

1558
Calais is taken by the French. Mary dies.
Elizabeth, daughter of Henry VIII and Anne Boleyn, becomes Queen Elizabeth I of England.

1559
Enthusiastic Protestant John Knox returns to Scotland from exile.
In England, the Book of Common Prayer once again becomes the only legal form of worship; the Catholic mass is henceforth illegal.

1562
Captain John Hawkins sells African slaves in the Caribbean.

1566
Murder of Rizzio, Mary, Queen of Scots' secretary, in the Palace of Holyrood, Edinburgh.

1567
Mary, Queen of Scots is imprisoned in Loch Leven Castle.

1568
Mary, Queen of Scots, defeated at the Battle of Langside, escapes to England.

1569
Northern rebellion in England.

1570
The Pope declares Queen Elizabeth a heretic and excommunicates her.

1572
Francis Drake raids the Spanish Main.

1576
Sir Martin Frobisher searches for the North West Passage.

1579-83
Rebellion in Ireland.

1580
Francis Drake returns to England having circumnavigated the world.

1583
University of Edinburgh founded.

1584
Colonisation of Virginia. Queen Elizabeth grants Walter Raleigh a charter authorising exploration and colonisation of remote, heathen and barbarous lands.

1586
Walter Raleigh introduces tobacco, maize and potatoes to Britain (it is possible that tobacco, at least, was known in this country before then).

1587
Execution of Mary, Queen of Scots at Fotheringhay Castle as a consequence of being implicated in the Babington Plot, one of several plans to assassinate Elizabeth and replace her with Mary.

1588
The Spanish Armada – an attempted invasion of England is thwarted by a combination of better leadership and bad weather.

c1590
First performance of Shakespeare's plays - possibly Henry VI, Parts 1, 2 and 3.

1600
British East India Company receives its charter.

1601
Earl of Essex rebellion

1603
Elizabeth dies. The English throne is offered to James VI of Scotland, who becomes James I of England and the first King of Great Britain.

VI STUART TIMELINE

1603
Scottish King James VI, son of Mary, Queen of Scots, becomes James I of England and the first King of Great Britain.

1604
James makes peace with Spain.

1605
The Gunpowder Plot – a foiled terrorist coup d'état by a group of Roman Catholics to blow up Parliament, murder the king, and replace him with his daughter, Elizabeth.

1607
Foundation of Jamestown, Virginia - the first permanent British colony in North America.

1609
The Plantation of Ulster - English and Scottish Protestants are encouraged to move to Ireland taking land confiscated from Catholics.

1610
The Newfoundland Company sets out to form a colony in Newfoundland.

1611
The King James Bible is published.

1616
William Shakespeare dies.

1618
Sir Walter Raleigh is executed.

1620
The Pilgrim Fathers sail to the New World.

1621
Oxford's Botanic Garden founded - Britain's oldest botanic garden.

1624-30
War with Spain.

1625
Barbados becomes a British colony.

1626-29
War with France.

1628
George Villiers, Duke of Buckingham, Charles I's unpopular chief minister, is assassinated in Portsmouth. William Harvey describes the circulation of blood in the human body.

1629
Charles I dissolves Parliament and rules without it for 11 years.

1630
Considerable emigration to Massachusetts Bay, particularly of fundamental Puritan Protestants.

1637
Charles I tries to force a new prayer book in Scotland, which is seen as an attempt to reintroduce Catholicism. In Oxford, the first coffee house in Britain opens.

1638
Scots draw up a 'National Covenant' to resist 'religious innovation' and demand a free Scottish parliament.

1640
Start of the Long Parliament.

1642
The start of the English Civil War between Parliament and the King. Charles I raises his standard at Nottingham.

1643
Alliance between the English and Scottish parliaments against the King.

1644
Parliament wins the Battle of Marston Moor. The King loses control of the North of England.

1645
Parliament's New Model Army wins the Battle of Naseby; the Royalist army is effectively destroyed.

1646
Charles I surrenders to the Scots.

1647
The Scots sell Charles to Parliament.

1648
2nd Civil War. Oliver Cromwell beats a Royalist army at Preston.

1649
The trial and execution of Charles I. England and Wales become a republic.

1649-50
Oliver Cromwell crushes resistance in Ireland, including the controversial sackings of Drogheda and Wexford.

1650-52
Cromwell crushes resistance in Scotland.

1651
Charles II is crowned King in Scotland - and defeated at the Battle of Worcester.

1652-54
1st Dutch War.

1652
Society of Friends (Quakers) is founded.

1653
Cromwell becomes Lord Protector.

1655
Jews are allowed to return to England. Britain takes Jamaica from Spain.

1658
Cromwell dies. The first tea is sold in Britain.

1660
Restoration of the Monarchy. The Royal Society is founded. And it's the year that Samuel Pepys started a diary.

1664
The British capture New Amsterdam and rename it New York (after the Duke of York, the future James II).

1665-67
2nd Dutch War. In 1667, the Dutch attack the Naval Dockyard at Chatham.

1665
The Great Plague of (mainly) London.
Robert Hooke discovers the cell.

1666
Great Fire of London – destroys most of the medieval city.

1667
John Milton publishes 'Paradise Lost'.

1669
Christopher Wren is given the job of designing a new St Paul's Cathedral.

1672-74
3rd Dutch War.

1673
The Test Act excludes Catholics from public office.

1678
Titus Oats and the Popish Plot – a fictitious plan to assassinate the king.
John Bunyan publishes 'Pilgrim's Progress'.

1679
The Act of Habeas Corpus guards against unlawful imprisonment.

1683
The Ashmolean Museum opens in Oxford - Britain's oldest museum.

1685
The Monmouth Rebellion – ends in failure.

1687
Isaac Newton publishes his theory of universal gravitation and three laws of motion.

1688
The 'Glorious Revolution' - William of Orange is invited to invade, lands a Dutch Army in Brixham and James II flees the country.

1689
The Bill of Rights establishes the principles of a constitutional monarchy.

1690
Battle of the Boyne. Ousted King James and his Catholics are beaten by King William and his Protestants.

1692
The massacre at Glen Coe.

1694
Foundation of the Bank of England.

1695
Foundation of the Bank of Scotland.

1698
The English Parliament opens the slave trade to all.

1698
The Scottish Darien Company attempts to establish the colony of Caledonia in Panama; its subsequent failure was a serious blow for Scotland.

1701-14
War of the Spanish Succession.

1701
Act of Settlement - determines that the next monarch will be a Protestant.

1704
Battle of Blenheim. Allied armies under the Duke of Marlborough decisively beat a combined French/Bavarian army.

1707
Act of Union between England and Scotland.

1709
Abraham Darby launches a new process to make cheaper iron products using coke.

1712
Thomas Newcomen's steam engine.

1713
Britain gains Gibraltar.

1714
Death of Queen Anne, the last Stuart monarch. She is succeeded by George, Elector of Hanover, who became George I.

VII GEORGIAN, or HANOVERIAN, TIMELINE

1714
German-speaking George, Elector of Hanover, becomes George I, King of Great Britain and Ireland.

1715
First Jacobite Rising – attempt to regain the throne for the Stuarts ends in failure.

1718
Transportation Act - Britain starts shipping convicts to its American colonies.

1720
South Sea Bubble - major financial crisis, many lose fortunes.

1721
Sir Robert Walpole becomes Britain's first 'Prime Minister' and also receives 10 Downing Street.

1723
George Frideric Handel is appointed Composer to the Chapel Royal

1738
David Hume publishes his Treatise on Human Nature.

1739
John Wesley's first sermon preached 'in the field' - the birth of Methodism.
The War of Jenkins' Ear - Anglo-Spanish naval war.
Highwayman Dick Turpin is hanged in York.

1740-48
The War of the Austrian Succession.

1743
Battle of Dettingen (Germany) - George II is the last reigning British monarch to lead troops into battle.

1744
First rules of golf are drawn up in Edinburgh.

1745
2nd Jacobite Rising - the '45 Rebellion - Bonnie Prince Charlie lands in Scotland to restore the Stuart monarchy. His rebel army gets as far as Derby before retreating.

1746
Battle of Culloden – the defeat of Bonnie Prince Charlie's rebellion. The Government acts harshly to prevent further Stuart/Catholic uprisings.

1750
Start of the Highland clearances.
The laws of modern cricket are developed at Hambledon Cricket Club, in Hampshire.

1751
Gin Act - attempts to regulate (and reduce) the sale of spirits.

1752
Britain adopts the Gregorian Calendar, replacing the old style Julian Calendar. Some protest at their 'loss of 11 days.'

1753
British Museum established.

1755
Samuel Johnson publishes A Dictionary of the English Language.
The Hellfire Club is founded.

1756-63
Seven Years War - global conflict with Britain, Prussia and other German states allied against France, Austria, the Holy Roman Empire, Russia, and Sweden.

1756
The Black Hole of Calcutta – following Bengali capture of a fort, British prisoners are herded into a tiny room, where most died.

1757
Battle of Plassey - the British East India Co captures Bengal.

1759
Annus Mirabilis - the Year of Victories - major successes, primarily against the French, including a naval victory in Quiberon Bay preventing a French invasion and the capture of Quebec.
Scots poet Robbie Burns is born this year.

1761
Opening of the Bridgewater Canal.

1764
James Watt develops his steam engine.

1768
The Royal Academy is founded.

Timelines

1768
Captain James Cook sets off on the first of three voyages of scientific discovery and exploration, to Pacific Islands, New Zealand and Australia.
In Edinburgh, Volume 1 of the Encyclopaedia Britannica is published.

1769
Richard Arkwright patents his spinning frame.
Wedgwood's Etruria factory opens in Stoke-on-Trent.
Both the Duke of Wellington and his French adversary, Napoleon Bonaparte, were born this year, on 1 May and 15 August, respectively.

1772
Milestone court case effectively makes slavery illegal in England and Wales.

1773
The Boston Tea Party

1775-83
American War of Independence (American Revolutionary War).

1774
Discovery of oxygen in Britain; it had previously been discovered in Sweden...

1776
Declaration of American Independence.
Adam Smith's Wealth of Nations is published.

1778
John Paul Jones invades England, landing at Whitehaven.

1780
The Gordon Riots - an anti-Catholic protest ends up in general violence and looting in London.

1781
A Colonial-French army defeats Government army at Yorktown, Virginia.

1783
The Peace of Paris results in the recognition of an independent United States of America. British loyalists and freed slaves are evacuated, many travelling to Canada. William Pitt the Younger becomes Britain's youngest Prime Minister (so far) at the age of 23.

1784
East India Act increases Government control in India.

1786
David Dale establishes New Lanark Mills with Richard Arkwright.

1787
Construction of the Royal Pavilion at Brighton, a seaside retreat for the Prince of Wales, commences.
The first convicts are transported to Australia, sailing from Portsmouth to Botany Bay.
The world's first iron boat is launched, on the River Severn.

1789
In a wider context – the start of the French Revolution.
The Mutiny on the Bounty.

1791
Thomas Paine's 'Rights of Man' is published.

1791
The official birth date of the Ordnance Survey, Britain's mapping system.

1792
Britain establishes Sierra Leone as a home for former slaves.

1793-1815
Napoleonic Wars

1795
Mungo Park explores the Gambia and Niger rivers.

1796
Joseph Turner exhibits his first painting at the Royal Academy, 'Fishermen at Sea'.

1798
Introduction of income tax.
Jenner publishes his findings on smallpox.

1799
Robert Owen moves to New Lanark Mills.
The Combination Act prohibits Trades Unions.

1801
Act of Union between Britain and Ireland and the first Parliament of the United Kingdom.
Britain's first census.

1805
Battle of Trafalgar - Nelson beats a combined French and Spanish fleet and establishes Great Britain as the premier naval power for the next 100 years.

1807
Abolition of the Slave Trade (but not slavery itself).

1811
Luddite Riots - textile machinery is sabotaged in Lancashire, Yorkshire and Nottinghamshire.
Jane Austen publishes 'Sense and Sensibility'.

1812-14
War between the USA and Great Britain – the British burn Washington in 1814.

1814
Walter Scott publishes his first novel, 'Waverley'.

1815
Introduction of the Corn Laws places tariffs on imported grain.
Battle of Waterloo - British and Prussian armies finally defeat Napoleon.
Humphrey Davy invents the safety lamp.

1819
Peterloo Massacre - troops kill 11 and injure some 500 during a peaceful protest in Manchester.
Stamford Raffles establishes a trading post on the Malay Peninsula, which became Singapore.
Queen Victoria and Prince Albert were both born this year, on 24 May and 26 August, respectively.

1821-23
Famine in Ireland.

1821
John Constable shows 'The Hay Wain' at the Royal Academy.

Timelines

1823
The game of rugby is born when William Web Ellis picks up the ball during a football match and runs with it.

1825
The world's first steam railway service opens between Stockton and Darlington.

1828
Burke and Hare are arrested for multiple murders in Edinburgh, their victims being intended for medical dissection. It was easier than digging up freshly buried corpses.

1829
Catholic emancipation - Catholics no longer banned from holding public office or attending university. Robert Peel founds the Metropolitan Police.

1830
Liverpool-Manchester Railway opens.

1831
Faraday discovers electromagnetic induction.

1832
Great Reform Act - abolished some 'rotten' boroughs - parliamentary constituencies where few people lived - created new constituencies for the growing urban areas and slightly extended the franchise.
Jeremy Bentham, responsible for the principle of 'the greatest happiness of the greatest number', dies.

1833
Factory Act restricts the working hours of women and children.

1833
Slavery Abolition Act abolishes slavery in most of Britain's colonies.

1834
The Tolpuddle Martyrs are sentenced to transportation for combining to campaign for better working conditions. The Poor Law Amendment Act establishes workhouses as the main means of providing welfare.

1835
Fox Talbot's first photographic negative.

1836
Birth of the Chartist Movement, with the aim of political reform and extending the franchise.

1837
Queen Victoria becomes queen at the age of 18.

VIII VICTORIAN TIMELINE

1837
Queen Victoria becomes queen at the age of 18.

1838
Worcestershire sauce is invented.
Charles Dickens' novel 'Oliver Twist' is published.
Railway line opens between Birmingham and London.

1839-42
First Opium War, caused by China very unfairly trying to abolish Britain's trade in the drug.

1839
1st Treaty of London - created an independent, and neutral, Kingdom of Belgium, guaranteed by the European powers, including Prussia and Britain.
Chartist riots in South Wales.

1840
Queen Victoria marries her cousin, Prince Albert of Saxe-Coburg and Gotha.
Introduction of the penny post.

1841
The first modern census records details of every member of a household.

1843
Launch of SS Great Britain, the first propeller-driven transatlantic steamship.
The world's first underwater tunnel opens, beneath the Thames between Rotherhithe and Wapping in London.

1844
Birth of the Cooperative Movement (now the largest funeral business in the UK).

1845-52
Irish potato famine. As many as 1 million may have died and up to 2 million more emigrated, mainly to the USA, England and Scotland.

1845
Friedrich Engels publishes 'The Condition of the Working Class in England'.

1846
Corn Laws are repealed - the price of bread gradually reduces.

1847
The world's first public zoo opens at Regent's Park, London.
The worlds first municipal park opens in Birkenhead.
'Jane Eyre' by Charlotte Brontë is published, under the pen-name of Currer Bell.

1848
Public Health Act - first step toward improvements in sewerage, food standards etc.
In a wider context - 1848 is often seen as a year of revolution, with widespread, seemingly disconnected and spontaneous, demonstrations in favour of increased democracy and liberalism in countries that included France, the Netherlands, German and Italian states, the Austrian Empire, Hungary, Poland and Denmark.

1849
The British conquer the Punjab.
Charles Dickens' novel 'David Copperfield' is published.

1851
Britain shows off to the world at The Great Exhibition in Hyde Park.
Sir Titus Salt builds Saltaire, a model village for his workers near Bradford.

1852
George Cayley designs a glider to take a pilot.
David Livingstone begins his first exploration of the interior of Africa.

1853
Infant vaccination is made compulsory.
The first post boxes appear in Britain, following trials in Jersey.
Elizabeth Gaskell publishes 'Cranford'.

1854-56
Crimean War - an alliance of Britain, France and Turkey combine against Russia.

1855
Henry Bessemer invents his converter, improving the mass production of steel.

1856
Institution of the Victoria Cross - Britain's highest award for military gallantry.

1857-58
The Indian Mutiny.

1858
The Great Stink of the Thames. Joseph Bazalgette resolves to create a sewer network for central London. The first transatlantic telegraph communication (using undersea cable).

1859
Charles Darwin publishes 'On the Origin of the Species'.
Alfred, Lord Tennyson starts to publish 'The Idylls of the King', retelling the legend of King Arthur and his knights.

1860
HMS Warrior is launched - Britain's first ironclad warship.

1860
Florence Nightingale sets up the Nightingale Training School at St. Thomas' Hospital, London.

1861-65
In a wider context – the American Civil War.

1861
Prince Albert dies.
Post Office savings scheme launched.

1863
First underground railway opens between Paddington and Farringdon Street, London.
Foundation of the Football Association and agreement on the rules of soccer.

1864
The Clifton Suspension Bridge opens.

Timelines

1865
Foundation of the Salvation Army.
Lewis Carroll (Charles Lutwidge Dodgson) publishes 'Alice's Adventures in Wonderland'.

1867
Joseph Lister writes about his theories on antiseptics.
2nd Reform Act means that 33% of all adult males in Britain are eligible to vote.
Karl Marx publishes Volume 1 of 'Das Kapital'.

1868
Trades Union Congress established.
The last public execution in Britain.

1869
The Suez Canal opens.
Tea clipper The Cutty Sark is launched.

1870
Education Act (Forster's Act) established a network of secular primary schools alongside existing sectarian schools to provide elementary edukation for all up to the age of 11.
The Married Women's Property Act allowed any money which a woman earned to be treated as her own property, and not her husband's.

1871
In a wider context - the unification of Italy and Germany (the latter following the defeat of France by Prussia in the Franco-Prussian War of 1870-71). Italy and Germany were each previously a series of smaller states.

1872
The secret ballot is introduced for elections.

1872
The first FA Cup Final - between Wanderers and the Royal Engineers (Wanderers won, 1-0).

1876
Scots-born Alexander Graham Bell invents the telephone (in the US).
The Plimsoll Line (suggested by Samuel Plimsoll) is introduced to prevent the overloading of ships.

1877
Victoria becomes Empress of India.
Britain annexes the Transvaal.

1878
Congress of Berlin - Britain leases Cyprus from Turkey.

1879
Zulu Wars - Battles of Isandlwana and Rorke's Drift.
Tay Bridge rail disaster - 75 die when bridge collapses in a storm due to faulty construction.

1880-81
1st Boer War.

1880
First house to be lit by electricity (Cragside in Northumbria).
Education Act made attendance at school compulsory for all.

1882
Britain occupies Egypt.
Phoenix Park murders - two Government officials stabbed to death by Irish revolutionaries in Dublin.

1882
In cricket, Australia beat England at the Oval - the birth of 'The Ashes' (of cricket).
A new Married Women's Property Act allowed married women in England and Wales to have complete personal control over all of their property.

1883
'Treasure Island' by Robert Louis Stevenson is published.
Death of Karl Marx in London - Marx had lived there since 1849.

1884
3rd Reform Act increases the franchise to roughly 60% of adult males.

1885
Death of Gordon at Khartoum.
Clamours for 'Home Rule' (independence) for Ireland.

1887
'A Study in Scarlet', the first novel featuring Sherlock Holmes, is published.

1888
The Whitechapel Murders and the start of the unsolved mystery of 'Jack the Ripper'.
Cecil Rhodes founds the De Beers Mining Company.
The strike of the London Match Girls – not just a bad pun, but also probably the first industrial action to capture the attention of the nation.

1889
London Dock Strike - succeeded in winning 'the docker's tanner' (sixpence per hour) and seen as a milestone in establishing unions of unskilled workers.
The first mosque to be built in Britain opens in Woking.

1890
The Forth Bridge opens.
During this decade, motor cars begin to appear on British roads.

1891
Education Act established free state school education.
The first international telephone service, between London and Paris.

1892
Kier Hardie becomes the first Labour MP (for West Ham).

1893
Foundation of the Independent Labour Party

1894
Rudyard Kipling's 'Jungle Book' is published.
Tower Bridge opens.

1895
Foundation of the National Trust.
Oscar Wilde is sentenced to two years hard labour for gross indecency.

1896
Italian Guglielmo Marconi sends his first wireless communication in England.

1897
Formation of the National Union of Women's Suffrage Societies.

1898
The Battle of Omdurman.
HG Wells publishes 'War of the Worlds', his 6th novel.

1899-1902
2nd Boer War.

1899
First performance of Edward Elgar's 'Enigma Variations'.

1901
Victoria dies; her eldest son becomes King Edward VII.

IX EDWARDIAN TIMELINE

1901
Seebohm Rowntree publishes 'Poverty, A Study of Town Life', which shocks the establishment.
Edward VII becomes King.
The first wireless transmission across the Atlantic is made, from Cornwall to Canada.

1902
Britain finally wins the Boer War, but the use of concentration camps has made Britain internationally unpopular.
Balfour's Education Act - placed the administration of all elementary schools in the hands of local education authorities and encouraged the development of secondary education.
The first Marmite factory was established in Burton upon Trent.

1903
The first 'Lib-Lab' Pact - does much to weaken the Liberal Party.
The Women's Social and Political Union (WSPU) was founded by six women, including Emmeline and Christabel Pankhurst.
In a wider context - Wilbur and Orville Wright make the first successful piloted powered flight at Kitty Hawk, USA.

1904
The Entente Cordial is signed between Britain and France.
J M Barrie publishes 'Peter Pan'.

1906
Liberals win General Election on a platform of social reform.
The world's most powerful battleship, HMS Dreadnought, is launched at Portsmouth.
In Manchester, Charles Stewart Rolls and Sir Frederick Henry Royce form Rolls-Royce Limited.
Edith Nesbit publishes 'The Railway Children'.

1907
Britain agrees 'spheres of influence' with Russia, forming the so-called Triple Entente of Britain, France and Russia - as opposed to the Triple Alliance of Germany, Austria and Italy (1882).
The Music Hall Strike - artistes campaign for better pay and conditions.

1908
Old age state pensions are introduced.
The Olympic Games are held in London.
Robert Baden-Powell wrote 'Scouting for Boys' - birth of the scouting movement.
Boys' story paper 'The Magnet' introduces the character of Billy Bunter, by author Frank Richards (real name Charles Harold St John Hamilton).
American Samuel Franklin Cody makes the first powered flight in Britain.

1909
Liberal Chancellor David Lloyd George introduces his 'People's Budget' to fund social reforms. The budget is rejected by the House of Lords, forcing a General Election.
American Harry Selfridge opens his department store on Oxford Street.
Frenchman Louis Blériot flies across the English Channel.

1910

The Sidney Street Siege takes place - gunfire on the streets of London as armed police and soldiers (with 'assistance' from Home Secretary Winston Churchill) confront revolutionary terrorists.

The 'People's Budget' is passed with the help of Labour and Irish Nationalist support in the House of Commons.

Edward VII dies; George V becomes King.

Suffragettes, imprisoned for offences such as wilful damage, begin to go on hunger strike; eventually, the authorities decide to force-feed them.

Tonypandy, South Wales - miners' strike turns violent. Home Secretary Winston Churchill is criticised by many for not sending in troops sooner to prevent looting and by others for allowing them to be sent at all.

1911

Parliament Act - the House of Lords loses its absolute power of veto over legislation passed by the House of Commons.

The Agadir Crisis - rebellion in Morocco sparks French interest; Germany sends a gunboat to protect German interests; Britain sends battleships to support the French.

Violence escalates during the Liverpool Dock Strike (one of a wave of strikes prior to WW1): many are injured, troops shoot dead two strikers and a warship patrols off the coast at Birkenhead.

Winston Churchill becomes First Lord of the Admiralty.

Government introduces national insurance and unemployment benefit, laying the foundations for the Welfare State.

1912

Captain Robert Falcon Scott reaches the South Pole, only to find that Norwegian Roald Amundsen got there first; Scott and his party perish on the return journey.

1912
The Government proposes Home Rule for Ireland: in response, protestants and unionists in Ireland form the Ulster Volunteer Force, threatening civil war.
The Royal Flying Corps is established.
RMS Titanic sinks with the loss of more than 1500 lives.
Coal miners stage a national strike.

1913
Emily Davison promotes the suffragette cause by throwing herself under the King's horse at the Epsom Derby and subsequently dies.
George Bernard Shaw's 'Pygmalion' premiers - in Austria.
D H Lawrence publishes 'Sons and Lovers'.

1914
Some army officers suggest they will mutiny if ordered to enforce Home Rule in Ireland.
On 28th June, Archduke Franz Ferdinand of Austria is murdered in Sarajevo, Austro-Hungary's response provokes a crisis which drags in the world powers, Germany invades Belgium and on 4th August the British Empire declares war on Germany. The First World War is underway.

X MODERN TIMELINE 1914-1945

1914
Lord Kitchener calls for 100,000 volunteers to join the British Army.
The British Expeditionary Force (BEF) engages the Germans in Belgium but is forced to retreat.
British and French armies hold the Germans on the Marne. Defensive lines appear, running from the North Sea to the Swiss Frontier; the British Army is based in northern France and Belgium, around Ypres.
British and Indian troops invade Mesopotamia (Iraq, Syria, Kuwait).
Scarborough, Whitby and Hartlepool are shelled by the Imperial German Navy.

1915
Zeppelins bomb King's Lynn, Great Yarmouth and London.
The Allies attack Gallipoli.
The 'shell crisis' (shortage of and faulty munitions) provokes a political crisis, leading to the formation of a coalition government.
RMS Lusitania is sunk by a German submarine with the loss of c1200 lives, including 128 Americans.
Allied troops land in Salonika.
British nurse Edith Cavell is executed by the Germans for espionage.
British Government representatives promise Arab leaders an independent Arab state in return for support against the Turks.

1916
Conscription is introduced.

Timelines

1916

Easter Rising in Dublin - Irish nationalist rebels take over key buildings; most of the leaders are executed.

Battle of Jutland - the only major naval engagement of the war.

Battle of the Somme - the British Army alone suffers almost 58,000 casualties on the first day, including 19,240 dead. Tanks are used for the first time.

Craiglockhart Hospital in Edinburgh is set up to deal with shell-shocked officers.

David Lloyd George becomes Prime Minister.

The Sykes-Picot agreement sets out to divide parts of post-war Middle East between France and Britain.

1917

Britain tells the US of German plans to bring Mexico into the war.

USA declares war on Germany.

King George V changes the Royal Family's name from Saxe-Coburg Gotha to Windsor.

New Zealander Harold Gillies pioneers plastic surgery in Sidcup.

Ernest Rutherford splits the atom.

British launch offensive at Messines and Passchendaele and, in the Middle East, capture Baghdad and Jerusalem.

Revolution in Russia results in withdrawal of Russia from the war and the formation of the Union of Soviet Socialist Republics (USSR), or 'Soviet Union'.

The Balfour Declaration confirms Britain's support for a 'national home' for the Jewish people in Palestine.

1918

Spring sees the outbreak of the influenza pandemic that went on to kill an estimated 50 million people worldwide, including more than 200,000 in Britain.

1918
The Royal Air Force is formed from the Royal Flying Corps and the Royal Naval Air Service.
The Germans launch a massive Spring Offensive, which pushes the Allies back on the Western Front.
Allied troops land in Murmansk in support of anti-Bolshevik forces.
The Allies, now reinforced by the USA as 'an associate power', eventually counter-attack and the Germans retreat, culminating in an armistice.
The Fourth Reform Act gives the vote to all men over 21 and, with certain restrictions, women over 30.

1919
The 'Battle of George Square' - massive strike in Glasgow leads to violence and troops being mobilised.
The Treaty of Versailles and the establishment of the League of Nations (forerunner of the UN).
Amritsar Massacre - British troops open fire on a crowd of unarmed Indian protestors, killing 300 and wounding hundreds more.
John Alcock and Arthur Brown make the first non-stop transatlantic flight.
Nancy Astor, Viscountess Astor, becomes the first woman to sit in the House of Commons.

1920
British take over governing Palestine and Mesopotamia (roughly modern Iraq, Syria and Kuwait).
Agatha Christie publishes 'The Mysterious Affair at Styles'.

1921
Irish Free State established, leaving the 6 counties of Ulster (Northern Ireland) as part of the UK.
Marie Stopes opens the first family planning clinic.

Timelines

1922
Civil War in Ireland.
First British Broadcasting Company radio broadcast; the current BBC (British Broadcasting Corporation) was formed in 1926.
In a wider context - Stalin becomes General Secretary of the Communist Party of the Soviet Union.

1923
Introduction of an annual licence fee for radios – it cost 10 shillings (50p).

1924
Britain's first Labour Government and Prime Minister, Ramsay Macdonald; the Conservatives won a landslide at the General Election later in the year.

1925
Plaid Cymru - the national party of Wales - is formed.
In a wider context - Mussolini becomes dictator of Italy - *Il Duce*.

1926
John Logie Baird demonstrates the first television.
The threat of lower pay and longer hours for coal miners results in the Trades Union Congress calling a General Strike.
Australia, New Zealand, Canada and South Africa are recognised as autonomous countries.
A A Milne publishes 'Winnie-the-Pooh'.

1928
All women over 21 get the vote.
The first 'talkie' film, 'The Jazz Singer', opens in London.
Alexander Fleming discovers Penicillin.

1929
Crash on Wall Street in the US leads to the Great Depression.

1931
Financial crisis leads to the formation of a National Government.
The world's first purpose-built recording studio opens in Abbey Road, London.
In a wider context - Japan invades Manchuria.

1932
A mass trespass by ramblers on Kinder Scout, Derbyshire, highlighted the lack of public access to the countryside in England and Wales.
Unemployment peaks at just under 3 million.

1933
In a wider context - Hitler comes to power in Germany.

1934
Scottish Nationalist Party is formed.

1935
Penguin paperback books go on sale (cost 6d – equivalent to 2.5p).
Robert Watson-Watt develops radar (he was supposed to be inventing a death-ray).

1936-39
In a wider context – the Spanish Civil War

1936
George V dies, Edward VIII abdicates in order to marry Wallis Simpson, George VI becomes King.
Start of regular TV broadcasts.

Timelines

1936
The Jarrow March - 200 men walk from NE England to London to highlight poverty and unemployment.

1937
J R R Tolkien publishes 'The Hobbit'.

1938
Munich Crisis – Prime Minister Chamberlain avoids war at the expense of an independent Czechoslovakia.
Kindertransports start to arrive in Britain; eventually, 10,000 Jewish children escaped the Nazis by coming to Britain, though most of their parents perished.

1939-45
Second World War.

1939
Germany invades Poland, Britain and France declare war on Germany.
The Bombe, an electro-mechanical machine to help break enemy codes, was designed by Alan Turing.

1940
Germany invades Denmark and Norway. Britain and France attempt to invade Norway, but are repulsed.
Italy declares war on France and Britain.
Winston Churchill becomes Prime Minister.
British and Allied troops evacuated from Dunkirk following the success of Germany's invasion of France and the Low Countries.
Germany occupies the Channel Islands.
The Battle of Britain takes place between fighters of the RAF and the German Luftwaffe over Southern England.
The Luftwaffe switches to bombing British cities - 'the Blitz' - mainly at night; it lasts until well into 1941.

1941
British and Australian troops push back Italians in North Africa, but are themselves forced to retreat when German troops under Rommel arrive.
Germany invades Greece, Yugoslavia and Crete.
The Royal Navy captures an 'Enigma' machine.
Britain's first jet aircraft flies.
Germany attacks the USSR.
Japan attacks the US base at Pearl Harbor, bringing the USA into the war, and simultaneously attacks Malaya and Hong Kong.

1942
The Fall of Singapore; about 85,000 British, Australian and Indian troops surrender to the Japanese.
US troops arrive in Britain.
The RAF starts bombing German cities.
The Battle of El Alamein pushes the Germans back in North Africa.
The Battle of Stalingrad – eventual Soviet victory is a turning point in the war.
Beveridge submits his report on social security, which forms the basis of Labour policy on the Welfare State.
Operation Torch - British-American invasion of French North Africa.
Enid Blyton publishes 'Five on a Treasure Island'.

1943
American-British invasion of Italy.
The Allies bomb Hamburg, unleashing a firestorm.

1944
Butler's 1944 Education Act raised the school-leaving age to 15 and provided universal free schooling in three different types of secondary school - grammar, secondary modern and technical – based on an examination, the 11+.

1944

D-Day landings in Normandy by American, British, Canadian, French and Polish troops.
The Germans launch V1 and V2 rockets against Britain and her allies.
Allied armies defeat the Japanese at Kohima and Imphal.

1945

The Yalta Conference determines the division of post-war Germany.
The Soviets liberate Auschwitz death camp.
British troops come across Bergen-Belsen concentration camp.
Soviet and American troops meet at the Elbe.
Germany surrenders unconditionally.
Labour win a landslide at the General Election, Churchill is beaten and Clement Atlee becomes Prime Minister.
The US drop atomic bombs on Japan.
The Soviet Union declares war on Japan.
Japan surrenders and the Second World War ends.
United Nations established.

XI MODERN TIMELINE 1945-2000

1945
End of the Second World War.
The Nuremberg Trials begin in Germany – a military tribunal convened by the victorious Allies (the UK, USA, USSR and France) to bring those deemed guilty of war crimes to justice.

1946
The Labour Government starts a programme of nationalising key businesses.
Winston Churchill makes his 'Fulton Speech' in the USA declaring that an Iron Curtain has descended across Europe.
A combined radio/TV licence is introduced, costing £2 a year.
Free milk is introduced for all school pupils under 18.

1947
The coal industry is nationalised.
Exceptionally harsh winter brings hardship for many.
India becomes independent and the separate state of Pakistan is created.

1948
Railways are nationalised.
The SS Empire Windrush docks at Tilbury from Jamaica, seen by some as the start of mass immigration from Britain's former imperial possessions.
Declaration of a Jewish state in Israel and British withdrawal from Palestine (precipitates Arab-Israeli War).
The National Health Service is launched.
The Berlin Airlift takes supplies to the city, blockaded by the Soviet Union.

Timelines

1948
Olympic Games held in London.

1949
The Yangtze River Incident - Royal Navy sloop HMS Amethyst comes under attack from the Chinese People's Liberation Army.
George Orwell (Eric Blair) publishes 'Nineteen Eighty-Four'.
Formation of NATO - The North Atlantic Treaty Organisation.

1950-53
Korean War.

1950
C S Lewis publishes 'The Lion, the Witch and the Wardrobe'.
Steel is nationalised – later reversed by the Conservatives.
The first British troops arrive in Korea; ultimately, up to 100,000 UK service personnel were deployed.

1951
Soviet spies, Burgess and Maclean, flee Britain.
The Conservatives win the General Election, remaining in power until 1964.
The UK's first National Park – the Peak District.
In a wider context - the European Coal and Steel Community, the forerunner of the European Economic Community, or Common Market (1957), is formed; its members are Belgium, France, Italy, Luxembourg, the Netherlands and West Germany.

1952
George VI dies; his daughter becomes Queen Elizabeth II.
London 'smog' kills 4,000 people.
Britain successfully tests an atom bomb in the Monte Bello Islands, Western Australia, and becomes the world's third nuclear power (after the United States and the Soviet Union).

1953
Ian Fleming publishes 'Casino Royale', the first James Bond book.
James Watson and Frances Crick determine the double-helix structure of DNA.
New Zealander Edmund Hillary and Nepalese Tenzing Norgay are the first to reach the summit of Everest.

1954
Roger Bannister runs a mile in under 4 minutes.
Rationing, in place since the Second World War, comes to an end.

1955
Commercial television begins.
Mary Quant opens her first shop, 'Bazaar', on Chelsea's Kings Road.
Ruth Ellis becomes the last woman to be hanged in Britain.
In a wider context – the USSR forms the Warsaw Pact, in response to NATO.

1956
The Clean Air Act aims to reduce pollution.
Calder Hall, Britain's first nuclear power station, opens.
Dodie Smith publishes '101 Dalmatians'.

Timelines

1956
Suez Crisis - Britain and France invade Egypt after the Suez Canal is nationalised, but are forced to withdraw under pressure from the USA.
Elvis Presley has his first hit in the UK, 'Heartbreak Hotel'.
Lonnie Donegan has his first hit, 'Rock Island Line'.
The government launches National Premium Bonds.

1957
The Gold Coast becomes the first African state to become independent of Britain; it is renamed Ghana.
Britain tests its first hydrogen bomb.
Malayan Independence follows a successful war (called 'emergency' for insurance purposes) against communist-led insurgents.
Prime Minister, Harold Macmillan, says that "most of our people have never had it so good".
In a wider context - The Treaty of Rome signed on 25 March 1957 by Belgium, France, Italy, Luxembourg, the Netherlands and West Germany created the European Economic Community.

1958
The Munich Air Disaster – 22 of 44 people on board BEA Flight 609 died as the aircraft fails to take-off. Fatalities include 8 members of Manchester United's football team, nicknamed 'the Busby Babes', as well as members of staff and journalists.
Britain's first motorway opens - the Preston by-pass, now a section of the M6.
The last debutantes were presented to the Queen.
Michael Bond publishes 'A Bear Called Paddington'.
Foundation of CND - the Campaign for Nuclear Disarmament.

1958
Tension between Teddy Boys and Jamaicans results in the Notting Hill race riots.

1959
The first Mini motor car rolls off the production line.
The Postmaster General introduces modern postcodes.
In a wider context – the first integrated circuit is patented in the US.

1960
Cyprus gains independence - following a conflict since 1955 against EOKA who wanted union with Greece and the Turkish Resistance Organisation, which opposed it.
The end of National Service (conscription); the last conscripts left the services in 1963.
Penguin Books is found not guilty under the Obscene Publications Act for publishing D H Lawrence's novel 'Lady Chatterley's Lover'.
The TV soap, 'Coronation Street', is broadcast for the first time.

1961
The Pill - the oral contraceptive pill - becomes available in Britain.
In a wider context – on 12th April, Russian Yuri Gagarin aboard Soviet spaceship Vostok 1 becomes the first man in space. And in August the GDR (German Democratic Republic of East Germany) starts building the Berlin Wall.

1962
The Beatles release their first single, 'Love Me Do', which gets to No 17 in the charts.
'Dr No', the first James Bond film, is released.
In a wider context – the Cuban Missile Crisis brings the world to the brink of nuclear war.

Timelines

1962
It is announced that Britain will buy Polaris nuclear missiles from the US.

1963
The Profumo Affair - a scandal erupts after it emerges that a government minister, John Profumo, has 'shared the affections' of a girl, Christine Keeler, with a Soviet diplomat.
Kim Philby, MI6 agent - the so-called 'Third Man' defects to the Soviet Union. The 'fourth man', Anthony Blunt, is identified but the fact is kept secret until 1979.
In a wider context – John F Kennedy, 35th President of the USA, is assassinated in Dallas, Texas.

1964
In the USA, 73 million people watch The Beatles perform on the Ed Sullivan Show.
The Rolling Stones have their first No 1, 'It's All Over Now'.
The last judicial hangings in Britain took place simultaneously on 13th August when Gwynne Evans was executed at Strangeways Prison, Manchester, and Peter Allen was executed in Walton, Liverpool, both for the murder of John West.
The Labour Party wins the General Election and Harold Wilson becomes Prime Minister.

1965
Abolition of the death penalty.

1966
Time magazine publishes an article about Swinging London. The model Twiggy is named "The Face of 1966". Britain's first credit card, Barclaycard, is launched.

1966
Aberfan disaster - the Welsh village of Aberfan was engulfed in tons of coal slag, killing 48 adults and 116 children, many in their classrooms.
England win the Football World Cup (and won't let anyone else forget it).

1967
Donald Campbell perishes attempting the World Water Speed Record on Coniston Water, driving Bluebird K7.
The Government nationalises the British Steel Industry.
The Beatles release 'Sergeant Pepper's Lonely Hearts Club Band'.
Homosexual acts in private between consenting men over the age of 21 are decriminalised in England and Wales.
Abortion becomes legal in the UK (except for Northern Ireland).
The BBC launches Radio 1 to win listeners from the popular pirate radio stations (which the Government has declared illegal anyway) and Radio Luxembourg.
The People's Republic of South Yemen (Aden) is declared following the withdrawal of British troops and a conflict which had lasted since 1963.

1968
Thousands demonstrate in London against US involvement in Vietnam.
The first Isle of Wight Festival.
The government ends free milk for secondary schools.

1969
The Beatles' last public performance - on the roof of their Apple building in London.
Drilling for North Sea Oil begins.
Concorde makes its maiden flight.

1969
Troops are sent to Northern Ireland to restore order amidst increasing sectarian violence.
The first broadcast of Monty Python's Flying Circus.
The voting age is lowered to 18.
In a wider context – the USA's Apollo 11 space mission landed the first two people on the Moon. Commander Neil Armstrong was the first person to walk on the Moon on 20 July.

1970
The first Glastonbury Festival.
The Conservatives win the general election and Ted Heath becomes Prime Minister.

1971
The first British soldier is killed by the IRA in Northern Ireland.
Decimal currency is introduced, replacing pounds, shillings and pence.
In a wider context - the first commercially available microprocessor is launched by Intel

1972
Bloody Sunday – British paratroopers kill 26 unarmed civilians during a protest march in Londonderry.
The IRA explodes a bomb in Aldershot, killing 7 people (six women and a Roman Catholic chaplain), the first of many Irish republican terrorist attacks on mainland Britain.
Ugandan dictator Idi Amin expels Ugandan Asians; many obtain refuge in Britain.
Philips launched their Model 1500 Video Cassette Recorder (VCR).

1973
The United Kingdom joins the European Economic Community.
Pink Floyd release 'Dark Side of the Moon'.

1974
The government introduces the 3-day week to conserve electricity during a miners' strike.
M62 coach bombing – 12 murdered by the IRA.
The general election in February results in a hung parliament. Labour form a minority government and Harold Wilson returns as Prime Minister.

1974
Soviet-made Lada motor cars appear on Britain's streets.
The winners of the Eurovision Song Contest, held in Brighton, are Swedish group Abba with 'Waterloo'.
The second general election of the year gives Labour a narrow majority.
The first McDonald's opens in Britain, in Woolwich.
Lord Lucan disappears.

1975
Margaret Thatcher defeats Edward Heath and becomes the first female leader of the Conservative Party.
Charlie Chaplin is knighted.
The European Space Agency is established.
In a referendum on continued membership of the European Economic Community, 67% vote to remain.
The sit-com 'Fawlty Towers' is broadcast for the first time.
The Sex Discrimination and the Equal Pay Acts become law.

1976
Financial crisis forces the Labour Government to seek help from the International Monetary Fund (IMF).

1977
More than 20 million tune in their TVs to watch Morecambe and Wise's Christmas Show.

1978-79
The 'Winter of Discontent' - strikes by petrol tanker and truck drivers, hospital staff, refuse collectors, health workers. Rats swarm round uncollected rubbish and in Liverpool the dead go unburied.

1978
The world's first 'in vitro' baby is born in Oldham.

1979
Conservatives win the General Election and Margaret Thatcher becomes Britain's first female Prime Minister. The IRA murders Lord Louis Mountbatten on holiday in Ireland and on the same day kills 18 British soldiers in an ambush at Warrenpoint, NI.

1980
The Housing Act of 1980 gives council house tenants the right to buy the houses they rent.

1981
Arrival of the first IBM personal computer.
The BBC demonstrates the new compact disc (CD).
Racial and other social tensions lead to riots in many of Britain's towns, especially Brixton (south London), Toxteth (Liverpool) and Moss Side (Manchester).

1981
Greenham Common - women begin a protest against the deployment of US cruise missiles in Britain; the protest lasted 19 years.

1982
The Falklands War – Britain retakes the Falkland Islands following Argentinean invasion.

1984
Mass coal miners' strike sees more violence in Britain. The IRA tries to murder the Cabinet by planting a bomb in the Grand Hotel, Brighton; five people are killed. Unemployment exceeds 3 million.

1985
First mobile phone in Britain. On New Year's Day 1985, Sir Ernest Harrison, chairman of Racal Vodafone, was called by his son Michael, who said: "Hi, it's Mike. Happy New Year. This is the first-ever call on a UK mobile network."
Live Aid Concerts - massive global fund-raising music concerts organised by Bob Geldof and Midge Ure in aid of Ethiopian famine relief.

1986
The City of London's 'Big Bang' - the deregulation of the securities market lead to a revolution in the financial services sector, significantly increasing London's status as a global financial centre.
The Government starts privatising nationalised companies, a policy designed to help create a property-owning democracy, produce capital to help reduce government expenditure and bring an end to subsidies.

1987
Barclays introduce Britain's first debit card.

1988
A terrorist bomb destroys Pan Am Flight 103 over Lockerbie. All 259 people on board, plus 11 on the ground, perish.

1989
Tim Berners-Lee invents the world wide web.
In a wider context - the fall of the Berlin Wall – the end of the Cold War?

1990
Margaret Thatcher resigns as Prime Minister and leader of the Conservative Party. She is replaced by John Major.

1991
Operation Desert Storm - the First Gulf War, the liberation of Kuwait following invasion by Iraq.

1992
British troops sent to Yugoslavia as part of the UN Protection Force.

1993
Launch of the European single market.
The Treaty of Maastricht creates the European Union from the European Economic Union.
The racially motivated murder of teenager Stephen Lawrence in London leads to the Macpherson report, which highlights institutional racism within the Metropolitan Police.

1994
The Channel Tunnel opens.
The Church of England ordains women priests.
In a wider context – Nelson Mandela becomes President of South Africa on 10 May.

1996
Dolly the Sheep, the world's first cloned mammal, is born in Edinburgh.

1997
Tony Blair leads Labour to victory in the General Election after 18 years of Conservative government.
Britain hands Hong Kong back to China.
Diana, Princess of Wales, is killed in a car crash in Paris.
Scotland and Wales vote in favour of national assemblies.
JK Rowling publishes 'Harry Potter and the Philosopher's Stone'.

1998
The Good Friday agreement provides a basis for peace in Northern Ireland.

1999
Kosovo Crisis – the RAF contributes to NATO bombing campaign and Britain sends troops as part of a peace-keeping force.
Former Warsaw Pact members, the Czech Republic, Hungary and Poland, join NATO.

2000
The predicted end of the world didn't happen.

Note on sources and further reading

A Bit About Britain's History has evolved over a fairly long period of time, rather than being specifically researched, planned and written as an academic book. The broad range of, numerous and mainly secondary, sources used include visits to historic sites, TV programmes, booklets, magazines, books – of course - and even my own, dusty, accumulated knowledge. The Internet is obviously an invaluable tool. I did find that I missed a book I had as a child, *A Pageant of History*, which has somehow disappeared, but confess to occasionally dipping into my small retained collection of *Ladybird* history books. Bamber Gascoigne's amazing *Encyclopaedia of Britain* is never far from my desk anyway.

There are several more detailed general histories of Britain available, of course. Simon Jenkins' *A Short History of England* is good and Neil Oliver's *A History of Scotland* is immensely readable. David Starkey's *Monarchy* TV series is available on DVD and is engaging, fascinating and informative. With regard to particular periods, personal favourites include: *In Search of the Dark Ages* by Michael Wood; Bede's *History of the English Church and People*; *A Brief History of the Tudor Age* by Jasper Ridley; *Civil War* by Peter Ackroyd; *Battles of Britain* by William Seymour; Andrew Marr's *The Making of Modern Britain* and *A History of Modern Britain*; Martin Gilbert's separate and incredibly thorough histories of the First and Second World Wars and pretty much anything published by Max Hastings. I referred to and acknowledge all of the above, and more.

About the author

Mike first learned history on his dad's knee and studied medieval and modern British and European history at university. He was planning on teaching it, but then drifted into a career running his own business instead. Often at his happiest with his nose in a history book, or exploring a historic site where the past is close, several years ago Mike began a blog – now an increasingly authoritative website – 'A Bit About Britain' (bitaboutbritain.com). He had to write a bit about Britain's history for the website, and it seemed only sensible to put the material into his first book, 'A Bit About Britain's History'.

Printed in Great Britain
by Amazon